英訳付き

ニッポンの名前図鑑

和服・伝統芸能

監修　市田ひろみ

An Illustrated Guide to
Japanese Traditional Clothing
and Performing Arts

Editorial Supervisor Ichida Hiromi

淡交社

はじめに

結婚式でよく見られる「アノ」黒い和服は、なんていう名前？
「隈取」って、どんなもの？
どうやって「袈裟」を英語で説明したらいい？

日本に暮らしていても、意外に知らない事物が身の回りに多く
あります。形を知っていても、名前がわからないモノ。名前を
聞いても、どんな形か想像できないモノ。名前と形を知ってい
ても、具体的に由来やいわれを説明できないモノ。さらに、それ
を英語で説明するなんて……。
近年では、「Kimono」や「Kabuki」といった日本語が外国の方に
も通じたり、英語辞書の中にも収録されるほど一般的になって
います。また、外国人旅行者が着物をきたり、歌舞伎などの伝統
芸能を鑑賞しに行くこともあります。和の文化が世界的に注目
されているにも関わらず、日本の事物を日本語でも英語でも説
明できないのは、日本人にとって心もとないことです。
本書では、「和服」「伝統芸能」にまつわるモノの名前を取り上げ
ました。日本人として知っておきたい代表的な名前を選び、和
名・英名、和名のローマ字表記を掲載し、いわれなどの詳細ま
で付しました。ただし、モノの名前には地域性があり、本書で紹
介するものがすべての地域に対応するわけではないことをご了
承ください。
これまで目をつぶってきた日本特有のモノを見つめ直しましょ
う。友人や外国の方にさらっと説明ができると、少し誇らしく
ありませんか？

Introduction

What is that black kimono you see at weddings called?
What exactly is *kumadori*?
And how can I explain *kesa* in English?

Even for Japanese, we find there are many things around us we don't actually understand well. Or perhaps, we know what something looks like, but can't remember what it's called. Other things we cannot even picture. And even for things we can easily identify, it is difficult to explain their origins.

Recently, Japanese culture has become so popular that more and more words like "Kimono" or "Kabuki" can be found in English dictionaries. It is no longer so rare for foreigners to wear kimono or go to see Japanese traditional performing arts like Kabuki. However, despite the international interest in Japanese culture, one may feel somewhat uneasy trying to explain these traditions in English.

This book is for those who wish to introduce Japanese culture in English as well as for foreigners who wish to learn more about Japanese traditions. This particular edition is a collection of things related to Japanese traditional clothing and performing arts. We have used the names that are most commonly used, described in Roman characters, and have provided English names as well as a description of their origins. It is worth noting the names may vary from one region to another.

We hope this book will be a helpful guide for understanding and explaining Japanese traditional culture to your friends and to people all around the world.

CONTENTS

和服
JAPANESE TRADITIONAL CLOTHING

着物の各部名称　Parts of Kimono

衿・eri 　12

重ね衿・kasane-eri／伊達衿・date-eri　袖・sode　袂・tamoto

おはしょり・ohashori　裾・suso 　13

掛衿・kake-eri／共衿・tomo-eri　衿先・eri-saki　裄・yuki 　14

袖付・sode-tsuke　振り・furi　身八つ口・miyatsuguchi

前身頃・maemigoro　衽・okumi　褄・tsuma／褄先・tsuma-saki

八掛・hakkake／裾回し・suso-mawashi 　15

着物の種類　Styles of Kimono

留袖・tomesode 　16

振袖・furisode 　17

訪問着・homongi 　18

付け下げ・tsukesage 　19

色無地・iromuji 　20

小紋・komon 　21

絣・kasuri 　22

浴衣・yukata 　23

帯の種類　Types of Obi

袋帯・fukuro-obi　名古屋帯・nagoya-obi

半幅帯・hanhaba-obi　角帯・kaku-obi／博多帯・hakata-obi 　25

帯の結び方　Obi Knots

太鼓結び・taiko-musubi　ふくら雀・fukura-suzume 　26

文庫・bunko　貝の口・kai no kuchi 　27

帯の小物　Obi Accessories

帯締め・obi-jime（丸組・平組）帯揚げ・obi-age（正絹・総絞り）28

帯留め・obi-dome 　29

和装の下着類　Related Garments for Kimono

長襦袢・naga-juban　肌襦袢・hada-juban	30
半衿・han-eri　伊達締め・datejime	31
帯板・obi-ita　帯枕・obi-makura	32
足袋・tabi	33

履き物　Footwear

草履・zori　駒下駄・koma-geta	34
のめり・nomeri／千両・senryo　雪駄・setta	35

和装の持ち物　Accessories

巾着・kinchaku	
合切袋・gassai-bukuro／信玄袋・shingen-bukuro	36
風呂敷・furoshiki　手拭い・tenugui	37
夏扇・natsu-ogi	39
祝儀扇・shugi-ogi／白扇・hakusen	
不祝儀扇・fushugi-ogi／喪扇・mosen	40
茶席扇・chaseki-ogi／茶扇子・cha-sensu	
舞扇子・mai-sensu／舞扇・mai-ogi	41

茶会の持ち物　Items for Tea Ceremony

帛紗（袱紗）・fukusa	
帛紗挟み・fukusa-basami／数寄屋袋・sukiya-bukuro	42
菓子楊枝と懐紙・kashiyoji and kaishi	43

色の名前　Japanese Colors

洗朱・araishu　紅色・kurenai-iro (beni-iro)	
唐紅色（韓紅色）・kara-kurenai-iro	44
臙脂色・enji-iro　黄丹・oni　弁柄色・bengara-iro	45
香色・ko-iro　山吹色・yamabuki-iro　鶯色・uguisu-iro	46
萌葱（萌黄）色・moegi-iro 若竹色・wakatake-iro 浅葱色・asagi-iro	47
藍色・ai-iro　縹（花田）色・hanada-iro　藤色・fuji-iro	48
江戸紫・edo-murasaki　利休鼠・rikyu-nezumi　鈍色・nibi-iro	49

伝統的な文様　Traditional Patterns

鱗・uroko　檜垣・higaki　網代・ajiro	50
亀甲・kikko　籠目・kagome　麻の葉・asanoha	51
紗綾形・sayagata　矢羽根・yabane　七宝繋ぎ・shippo-tsunagi	52
立涌・tatewaku　雷・rai　青海波・seigaiha	53

縞模様　Stripes

千筋・sen-suji　万筋・man-suji　大名筋・daimyo-suji	54

棒縞・bo-jima　矢鱈縞・yatara-jima　よろけ縞・yoroke-jima　　55

格子模様　Grids

市松模様・ichimatsu-moyo　障子格子・shoji-goshi

三筋格子・misuji-goshi　　56

弁慶格子・benke-goshi　業平格子・narihira-goshi

翁格子・okina-goshi　　57

家紋　Family Crests

五三ノ桐・gosan no kiri　蔦・tsuta　桔梗・kikyo　　58

揚羽蝶・agehacho　丸に剣片喰・maru-ni-kenkatabami

丸に九枚笹・maru-ni-kumaizasa　　59

丸に隅立四ツ目・maru-ni-sumitate-yotsume

丸に三ツ柏・maru-ni-mitsugashiwa

丸に橘・maru-ni-tachibana　　60

丸に違い鷹羽・maru-ni-chigai-takanoha

丸に梅鉢・maru-ni-umebachi　丸に横木瓜・maru-ni-yoko-mokko　61

婚礼の装束　Wedding Attire

白無垢・shiromuku　　62

打掛・uchikake　掛下・kakeshita

文金高島田・bunkin-taka-shimada　末広・suehiro　　63

紋付羽織袴・montsuki-haori-hakama　　64

紋・mon　羽織・haori　羽織紐（白房付き）・

haori-himo (shirofusa-tsuki)　馬乗袴・umanori-bakama　　65

社寺の装束　Priest Attire

［僧侶の装束］　袈裟・kesa　直綴・jikitotsu　中啓・chukei

　　　　　　　作務衣・samue　　67

［神職の常装］　狩衣・kariginu　烏帽子・eboshi　　68

　　　　　　　差袴・sashiko／切袴・kiri-bakama　笏・shaku

［巫女の装束］　緋袴・hi-bakama　上指糸・uwasashi-ito

　　　　　　　白衣・hakue (byakue/shirokinu)　　69

伝統行事の装束　Attire for Traditional Events

［力士の装束］　化粧回し・keshomawashi　　70

［行司の装束］　直垂・hitatare　侍烏帽子・samurai-eboshi

　　　　　　　軍配団扇・gunbai-uchiwa　　71

［祭り衣装］　鉢巻・hachimaki　袢纏・hanten　　72

　　　　　　　地下足袋・jika-tabi　草鞋・waraji

　　　　　　　腹掛け・haragake　股引・momohiki　　73

伝統芸能
JAPANESE TRADITIONAL PERFORMING ARTS

能装束　Noh Costumes

［女性の出立］唐織・karaori　摺箔・surihaku　鬘帯・kazura-obi　77

［舞の出立］長絹・choken　縫箔・nuihaku　胸紐・munehimo

菊綴・kikutoji　79

［武将の出立］法被・happi　厚板・atsuita

半切・hangire (hangiri)　腰帯・koshi-obi

梨子打烏帽子・nashiuchi-eboshi　81

［老人の出立］水衣・mizugoromo　尉髪・jogami　83

能面　Noh Masks

小面・ko-omote　深井・fukai　84

痩女・yase-onna　姥・uba　85

翁・okina／白式尉・hakushikijo　般若・hannya　86

飛出・tobide　大癋見・obeshimi　87

能舞台　Noh Stage

本舞台・hombutai　階・kizahashi　88

橋掛り・hashigakari　見所・kensho　89

［本舞台］鏡板・kagami-ita　シテ柱・shite-bashira

ワキ柱・waki-bashira　目付柱・metsuke-bashira

笛柱・fue-bashira　91

［橋掛り］一の松・ichi no matsu　二の松・ni no matsu

三の松・san no matsu　92

揚幕（能）・agemaku　93

囃子方・hayashikata　地謡・jiutai　94

後見・koken　作り物・tsukurimono　切戸口・kiridoguchi　95

能の楽器　Noh Instruments

太鼓・taiko　96

笛・fue／能管・nokan　97

小鼓・kotsuzumi　98

大鼓・otsuzumi　99

雅楽の装束　Gagaku Attire

［襲装束］袍・ho　半臂・hampi　指貫・sashinuki

踏懸・fugake　糸鞋・shikai　鳥甲・torikabuto　101

目次

7

[蛮絵装束]表袴・uenohakama　下襲・shitagasane
　　　　　巻纓冠・ken-ei no kan　緌（老懸）・oikake　　103
[別装束]　襦袢・ryoto　当帯・ate-obi
　　　　　陵王面・ryo-o-men　牟子・mushi　　　　　105

雅楽の楽器　Gagaku Instruments

篳篥・hichiriki　笙・sho　　　　　　　　　　　　106
高麗笛・komabue　龍笛・ryuteki　　　　　　　　107
楽箏・gakuso　爪・tsume　　　　　　　　　　　　108
楽琵琶・gakubiwa　　　　　　　　　　　　　　　109
鉦鼓・shoko　　　　　　　　　　　　　　　　　　110
釣太鼓・tsuri-daiko／楽太鼓・gaku-daiko　　　　111

文楽人形と人形遣い　Bunraku Puppet and Puppeteers

文楽人形・bunraku-ningyo　主遣い・omo-zukai　　112
舞台下駄・butai-geta　左遣い・hidari-zukai
足遣い・ashi-zukai　黒衣・kurogo　　　　　　　113

文楽の舞台　Bunraku Stage

太夫・tayu　三味線（文楽）・shamisen　見台・kendai　114
床・yuka　御簾・misu　　　　　　　　　　　　　115

歌舞伎の装束　Kabuki Costumes

[つっころばし]　着流し・kinagashi　丁髷・chon-mage
　　　　　　　鬢・bin　しけ・shike　　　　　　117
[武士]　　　　裃（上下）・kamishimo
　　　　　　　長袴・naga-bakama／引袴・hiki-bakama
　　　　　　　隈取・kumadori／むきみ隈・mukimi-kuma　119
[腹出し]　　　赤っ面・akattsura　着肉・chakuniku
　　　　　　　肉襦袢・niku-juban　三里当て・sanriate
　　　　　　　板鬢・ita-bin　　　　　　　　　　121
[赤姫]　　　　しごき帯・shigoki-obi／抱え帯・kakae-obi
　　　　　　　丸ぐけ・maruguke
　　　　　　　吹き輪銀の前ざし・fukiwa gin no maezashi　123
[町娘]　　　　黄八丈・kihachijo　黒衿・kuro-eri
　　　　　　　ふき綿・fukiwata　振り下げ・furisage　125
[花魁]　　　　まないた帯・manaita-obi　道中着・dochugi
　　　　　　　鼈甲の髪飾り・bekko no kamikazari
　　　　　　　三歯下駄・samba-geta　　　　　　127

歌舞伎の髪飾り　Kabuki Hair Ornaments

結綿・yuiwata　　　　　　　　　　　　　　　　128

元結・mottoi (motoyui)　丈長・takenaga

つまみ簪・tsumami-kanzashi　　　　　　　　129

角隠し・tsunokakushi／揚帽子・age-boshi

紫帽子・murasaki-boshi　　　　　　　　　　130

紫鉢巻・murasaki-hachimaki　病鉢巻・yamai-hachimaki　131

歌舞伎の舞台　Kabuki Stage

廻り舞台・mawari-butai　書割・kakiwari　　　132

遠見・tomi　引幕・hikimaku／定式幕・joshikimaku　133

［上手］　　上手・kamite　　　　　　　　　　134

　　　　　竹本・takemoto　ちょぼ床・choboyuka

　　　　　揚幕（歌舞伎）・agemaku　　　　　　135

［下手］　　下手・shimote　　　　　　　　　　136

　　　　　黒御簾・kuro-misu　花道・hanamichi

　　　　　迫り・seri　すっぽん・suppon　　　137

歌舞伎の小道具　Kabuki Props

煙管・kiseru　煙草入れ・tabako-ire　煙草筒・kiseru-zutsu　138

煙草盆・tabako-bon　灰吹・haifuki　火入・hi-ire　139

印籠・inro　根付・netsuke　　　　　　　　　140

筥迫・hakoseko　十手・jitte　　　　　　　　141

番傘・bangasa　　　　　　　　　　　　　　142

蛇の目傘・janomegasa　　　　　　　　　　　143

合掌鏡台・gassho-kyodai　角火鉢・kaku-hibachi　144

すし桶・sushi-oke　酒樽・saka-daru　　　　　145

歌舞伎の楽器　Kabuki Instruments

三味線・shamisen　　　　　　　　　　　　　146

びんざさら・binzasara　艪の音・ro no oto　　147

笏拍子・shaku-byoshi　盤木・bangi　　　　　148

雨団扇・ame-uchiwa　がり時計・garidokei　　149

日本の時代区分　Japanese Time Periods　　　　74

索引（五十音順）　Index for Japanese　　　　　150

本書の英訳について

1. モノ・コトの名前には、基本的に読み方（ヘボン式ローマ字表記）と英語名を掲載しています。英語名は必ずしも定型表現ではなく、場合によっては英語名を掲載していないこともあります。
2. 日本語の説明文と、英語の説明文とが対応していない場合（英訳では解説を割愛した箇所）があります。
3. 英訳文の中で、日本語読みのまま使用していることばは、イタリック（斜体）表記にしていますが、Oxford Advanced Learner's Dictionary 9th edition に英語として登録されていることばは正体にしております。
4. 能、雅楽、文楽（人形浄瑠璃）、浄瑠璃（義太夫）、田楽、歌舞伎といった単語の英語表記は、すべて正体に統一しています。
5. 長さは基本的にヤードポンド法で表記しています。1 inch (in.) = 2.5 cm、1 feet (ft.) = 12 in. = 30 cm で換算が可能です。
6. 日本の時代表記（平安時代、江戸時代など）が何世紀に相当するかについては、74頁をご参照ください。

About the Translation

1. The pronunciation of Japanese words in this book is written in the Hepburn Romanization system. Please note the English names may not necessarily be a fixed translation.
2. Some names and descriptions have not been translated from Japanese to English if they are not relevant to a non-Japanese audience.
3. Original Japanese words are italicized, except those listed in the Oxford Advanced Learner's Dictionary 9th edition.
4. Types of Japanese traditional performing arts such as Noh, Gagaku, Bunraku (Ningyo Jyoruri), Jyoruri (Gidayu), Dengaku and Kabuki are unitalicized.
5. Notation for lengths is in the imperial system. 1 inch (in.) = 2.5 cm、1 feet (ft.) = 12 in. = 30 cm
6. To convert Japanese time periods such as the Heian and Edo period to centuries, please refer to page 74.

和服

JAPANESE TRADITIONAL CLOTHING

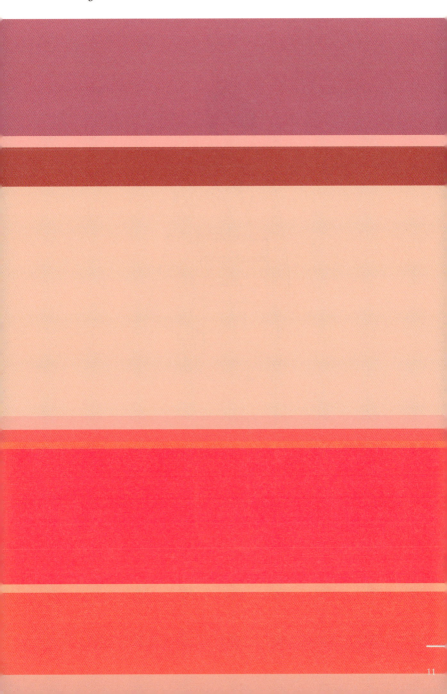

着物の各部名称

着物の形は決まっていて、女性用で幅約37cm、長さ約12mの長い布（着尺／きじゃく）を各パーツに直線裁ちしたものを組み合わせてつくられる。

半衿・*han-eri*
→ p. 31

帯揚げ・*obi-age*
→ p. 28

帯・*obi*
→ p. 24

帯締め・*obi-jime*
→ p. 28

足袋・*tabi*
→ p. 33

草履・*zori*
→ p. 34

1

衿・*eri*

Collar

着物の衿は、右→左の順に重ねる。これを「右前」という。

Worn with the left side over the right. This standard style is called *migimae*.

Parts of Kimono

Kimono have a T-shape, consisting of strips of fabric that are all cut along straight lines from a single bolt of fabric, about 15 in. wide and 39 ft. long for women.

2
重ね衿・*kasane-eri*／伊達衿・*date-eri*
Layered Collar

半衿（31頁）の上に重ねる色柄付きの布。礼装や晴れ着の際に用いる。

Colored and designed pieces of fabric layered over *han-eri* (page 31). Worn for formal and ceremonial occasions.

3
袖・*sode*
Sleeves

一般的な袖丈は約49cm。それより長い着物を「振袖」（17頁）という。

Standard length is about 19 in. Sleeves longer than that are called *furisode* (page 17).

4
袂・*tamoto*
Bottom Ends of Sleeves

袖の垂れ下がった部分のことで、袋状になっている。

Pouched and hung.

5
おはしょり・*ohashori*
Tuck

自分の着丈より長く余った分を、腰の辺りでたくし上げること。もしくはその部分。紐で締めて、長さを調節する。江戸時代頃まで、おはしょりをつくる風習はなかった。

Part to adjust hemline. By tying with a string, one can change the length of the kimono.

6
裾・*suso*
Hem

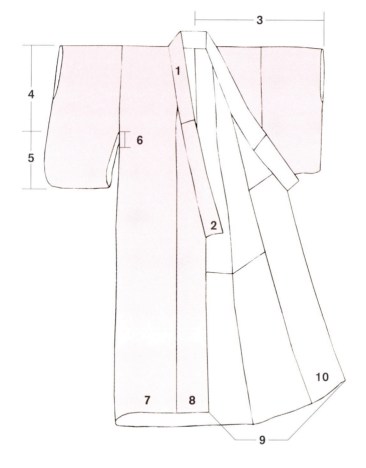

1
掛衿・*kake-eri* ／ 共衿・*tomo-eri*

着物の衿部分に別の布を掛けて、衿汚れを防いだもの。現在は、着物と同じ布をつけて仕立てるので「共衿」ともいう。

Cover to protect collars from staining. When the fabric is the same as the kimono, it's called *tomo-eri*.

2
衿先・*eri-saki*

3
裄・*yuki*

背中の中心から、袖口までの長さ。

Length between the center of the back and the end of the sleeve.

——4
袖付・*sode-tsuke*

袖部分のうち、身頃（みごろ）に縫い付けられている部分。
Part of the sleeves that are sewed onto the body.

——5
振り・*furi*

袖部分のうち、身頃に縫い付けられず、離れている部分。
Part of the sleeves that are not sewed onto the body.

——6
身八つ口・*miyatsuguchi*

袖付の下の、身頃側の開口部。
Openings under the *sode-tsuke*.

——7
前身頃・*maemigoro*

体の前面にくる袖と衽の間部分。背面を「後ろ身頃」と呼ぶ。
Front main panels. Back main panels are called *ushiromigoro*.

——8
衽・*okumi*

前身頃と衿につながる半幅の部分。
Half width strips connecting *maemigoro* and the collar.

——9
褄・*tsuma*／褄先・*tsuma-saki*

着物の両端の衿下あたりを「褄」、その最下方を「褄先」という。
Both sides of a kimono are called *tsuma* and the tips of the *tsuma* are *tsuma-saki*.

——10
八掛・*hakkake*／裾回し・*suso-mawashi*

着物の胴から裾にかけてつける裏地。「八掛（はっかけ）」の語源は、着物の八箇所につけることから。
Lining fabric attached to the bottom half of a kimono.

着物の種類

着物の着尺（きじゃく）には染物と織物がある。それぞれに多様で、TPOに合わせて着分ける。季節によっても異なり、袷（あわせ）、単衣（ひとえ）、薄物（うすもの）がある。

留袖・*tomesode*
Formal Kimono for Married Women

上半身は無地で、裾に模様が入った着物。地色が黒のものを「黒留袖」、黒以外のものを「色留袖」という。紋を5つつけた黒留袖は、結婚式で新郎新婦の母や親族が着る第一礼装。色留袖は一つ紋か三つ紋をつけて、準礼装にする。

Single-color kimono, patterned only below the waistline. Black kimono is called *kuro-tomesode* and other colors are *iro-tomesode*. *Kuro-tomesode* with five family crests is the most formal kimono for married women and often worn by the mothers of the bride and groom at a wedding. *Iro-tomesode* may have one or three family crests and is worn as a semi-formal kimono.

Styles of Kimono

There are two types of kimono fabric – dyed and woven. Each type varies in its designs and patterns and people choose what to wear according to the occasion. To match seasonal occasions, there are *awase*, lined kimono, *hitoe*, unlined kimono, and *usumono*, a semi-translucent fabric.

振袖 · *furisode*

Formal Kimono for Unmarried Women

袖丈を1m以上の長さにした未婚女性の第一礼装。華やかな柄物が多く、現在では成人式や卒業式によく着られる。

This is the most formal kimono for unmarried women with the sleeves that are longer than 3 ft. 3 in. Colorful patterns are common and people often wear it at coming-of-age or graduation ceremonies today.

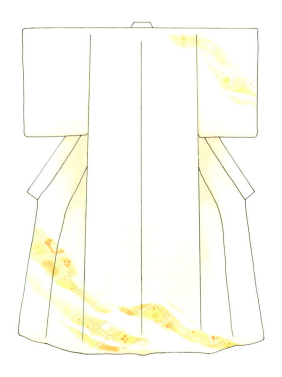

訪問着 · *homongi*
Semi-formal Kimono

着物全体に柄が入った華やかな着物。白生地を裁断して仮仕立てをしてから模様付けをする「絵羽（えば）模様」なので、各パーツの模様が縫い目で途切れず連続しているのが特徴。紋をつけなくても準礼装になり、留袖（16頁）の次に格が高い。

Colorful patterns cover the entire garment. Since the patterns are applied after the kimono is tacked, it is characterized by patterns that flow over the shoulders, seams and sleeves. It can be semi-formal wear without family crests and is the second most formal kimono after *tomesode* (page 16).

付け下げ・*tsukesage*
Informal Kimono

左右の身頃(みごろ)や肩、袖などに模様が入った着物。模様付けをする前に仮仕立てをしないため、模様が連続しないことがある。訪問着の略式として誕生したため、略礼装となる。

More modest patterns cover a smaller area such as the *migoro*, shoulders or sleeves. Skipping the process of tacking, patterns may not flow over seams. It is a simplified version of *homongi*.

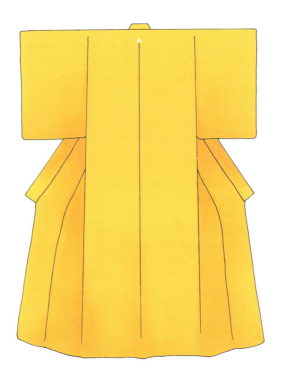

色無地 · *iromuji*

Single-colored Kimono

地紋がある、もしくは地紋のない生地を一色で染めた着物。礼装になるが、紋の数や合わせる帯（24頁）・小物（28頁）によって格が変わる。控えめな装いのため、茶会の着物として好まれている。

It is formal wear but its rank depends on the number of figures on the fabric or accompanying accessories (page 28) including the obi (page 24). The dyed fabric is not necessarily figured. Due to its modest aesthetic, people wear it to tea ceremonies.

小紋 • *komon*

Finely Patterned Kimono

型紙を使って着尺（きじゃく）全体に細かい模様が染められた着物。植物模様や幾何学的な模様もある。一般的な小紋は外出着で、礼装向きではない。

Using paper templates, fine detailed patterns cover the entire garment. Flower and plants or geometric patterns are common. This style is more casual and not suitable as formal wear.

絣 · *kasuri*
Ikat Kimono

経糸か緯糸、もしくはその両方を部分的に染めた「絣糸」を使って織った着尺(きじゃく)による着物。もしくはその模様のことをいう。柄は幾何学的なものから、絵を表す「絵絣」もある。糸の色がかすれて見えることから名が付いた。

Made of fabric that has been woven with the warp and weft threads partly dyed to create certain patterns or images in the fabric. Patterns vary from geometric figures to particular images. The name comes from *kasureru* which means scratchy in Japanese.

浴衣 · *yukata*

Casual Summer Kimono

夏に着る木綿製、型染の着物。現在は化繊のものも多い。その語源は「湯帷子（ゆかたびら）」で、帷子は裏地のない着物のこと。江戸時代に風呂の湯上り着として流行したことからのネーミング。

Traditionally made of silkscreened cotton but today synthetic fabrics are also available. The name comes from the unlined garment worn after bathing from the Edo period. *Yu* means hot water in Japanese.

帯の種類

帯とは、着物の上から腰に巻いて結ぶ細長い布のこと。通常の帯幅は30cm程度で、長さは種類によって異なる。着物の格と色合いなどを考えながら帯を選ぶことが、和装の要となる。

1

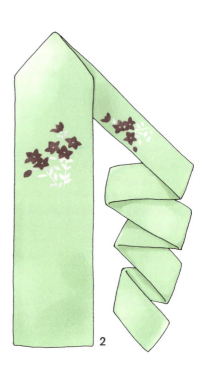

2

3

4

Types of Obi

Obi is a sash for kimono. Normally it is about 1 ft. wide and the length depends on the type of obi. It is critical with Japanese garments to choose the appropriate obi according to the rank and color of the kimono.

1

袋帯 · *fukuro-obi*
Formal Obi

礼装、準礼装などの着物に締めて、二重太鼓（太鼓結び・26頁）や変わり結びにする格の高い帯。袋のように筒型に織られたことから名が付いたが、現在は表地と裏地とが袋状に縫い合わされている。

Worn with formal and semi-formal kimono. One can make a *nijudaiko* knot (*taiko-musubi* /page 26) or *kawari-musubi* with this classy obi. The name comes from the fact it used to be woven into a pouch shape, *fukuro* in Japanese. Today, it is made by sewing two pieces of cloth together.

2

名古屋帯 · *nagoya-obi*
Semi-formal or Casual Obi

太鼓結び（一重太鼓）にするための帯。袋帯より70cmほど短い。手先（帯の端）と胴に巻く部分をあらかじめ半分に折って結びやすくした「名古屋仕立て」が一般的。名古屋で誕生したとされる。

2 ft. 4 in. shorter than *fukuro-obi*, it is suitable for making a *taiko-musubi* knot. Usually one end is folded and sewn in half.

3

半幅帯 · *hanhaba-obi*
Half-width Obi

帯幅が通常の半分（約15cm）になる帯。主に浴衣（23頁）や日常のおしゃれ着に合わせる。貝の口（27頁）や蝶結びで結ばれることが多い。

It is about 6 in. wide and worn with a *yukata* (page 23) or an everyday kimono. Usually worn with a *kai no kuchi* (clam's mouth) knot (page 27) or *chocho* (butterfly) knot.

4

角帯 · *kaku-obi* ／ 博多帯 · *hakata-obi*
Men's Obi

男性用の帯。幅は約10cm。貝の口で結ばれることが多い。イラストは「博多帯」といって、福岡県博多地区の特産品。

At about 4 in. wide, it is usually worn with a *kai no kuchi* knot. The illustration shows a *hakata-obi*, a specialty from Hakata, Fukuoka.

帯の種類　Types of Obi

和服

帯の結び方

帯の結び方にはいろいろあるが、現在の女性の外出着には太鼓結びを合わせるのが基本。振袖（17頁）などには、華やかな形の変わり結びにすることも多い。ここでは代表的なものを紹介する。

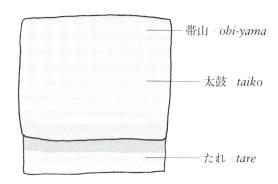

太鼓結び・*taiko-musubi*

袋帯や名古屋帯（25頁）の基本的な結び方。袋帯は長いため、お太鼓の部分の帯を二枚重ねて「二重太鼓」にする。

This is the standard knot for formal *fukuro-obi* and semi-formal *nagoya-obi* (page 25). *Fukuro-obi* is longer than other obi, so a *nijudaiko* (two-layer) knot is used by folding obi in two during the tying of the knot.

ふくら雀・*fukura-suzume*

袋帯の代表的な変わり結び。左右に羽根が出たところを、ふっくら太った雀に見立てた名前。

This is a typical variation for the *fukuro-obi*. The decorative knot resembles a sparrow with its wings spread.

Obi Knots

There are hundreds of decorative knots, but the *taiko-musubi* is the most common way of tying an obi for everyday kimono today. Usually, more decorative knots are used for *furisode* (page 17) and other formal kimono.

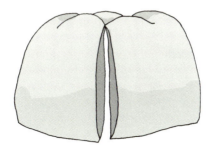

文庫 · *bunko*

半幅帯（25頁）で、二枚の羽をたらすように結ぶ、変わり結びの一種。
A variation for *hanhaba-obi* (page 25), with the wings folded down.

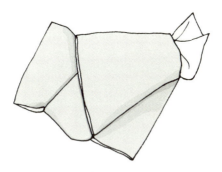

貝の口 · *kai no kuchi*

半幅帯や角帯（25頁）の最も一般的でシンプルな結び方。折り目が二つ重なっているかたちが、貝の口に似ていることから名が付いた。
The simplest and most common knot for *hanhaba-obi* and *kaku-obi* (page 25). The double folded shape resembles the mouth of a shell which, in Japanese, is *kai no kuchi*.

帯の小物

帯を締める際に用いられる小物を紹介する。それぞれに多様な種類や柄があり、帯や着物との調和を考えて用いる。

丸組・*marugumi*
Round *Obi-jime*

平組・*hiragumi*
Flat *Obi-jime*

帯締め・*obi-jime*
Obi Belt

帯がゆるまないように、帯の上から締める紐のこと。数本の糸を束にして編み上げられたものが多く、これを「組紐」という。平組、丸組、角組などの種類がある。

A string tied around the obi to prevent it from coming loose, which also doubles as decoration. Strings are usually woven and called *kumi-himo*. There are flat, round and square *obi-jime*.

正絹・
shoken
Pure Silk

総絞り・
soshibori
All Tie-dye

帯揚げ・*obi-age*
Obi Bustle

太鼓結び（26頁）をするときに、帯山が崩れないようにするために用いる布。帯の前上で結び、帯の中に収める。正絹製や絞り製がある。

This is a piece of cloth to keep the upper part of the *taiko-musubi* (page 26) knot in place. Tie it in front and above the obi, then tuck it in the obi. It is often made from silk and tie-dye fabric.

Obi Accessories

There are a variety of items to accessorize obi. Each accessory has a range of types and designs. One selects the appropriate items in harmony with the type of obi and kimono.

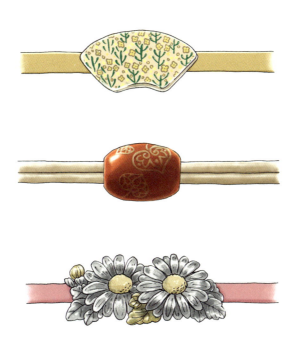

帯留め · *obi-dome*
Obi Clip

帯締めにつける飾り。彫金や宝石、陶器など多様な帯飾りがある。帯留めをつけた細い組紐は、結び目をお太鼓の中に入れ、飾りを正面にする。

A decorative accessory fastened onto the *obi-jime*. It can be made of metal, jewels or ceramics. Some *obi-jime* have *obi-dome* embedded in them.

和装の下着類

着物を着付ける際には、着物や帯まわりのもの以外にも、さまざまな小物や下着が必要となる。ここでは必要最小限のものを紹介する。

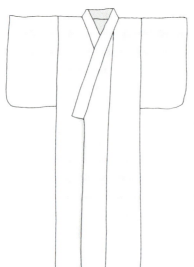

長襦袢・*naga-juban*

着物の下に着る衣類。丈は、着物と違って対丈（ついたけ／自分の背丈と同寸）に仕立てる。

A robe worn beneath the main outer garment. Unlike kimono, the length is made to fit one's height.

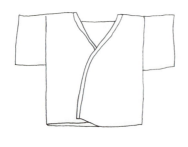 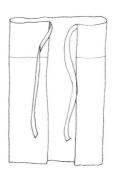

肌襦袢・*hada-juban*

長襦袢（ながじゅばん）の下に着る肌着。上半身と下半身で分けられている肌襦袢もあり、その場合に腰に回すものを「裾よけ」という。

Worn under *naga-juban*, some are separated and the ones similar to half-slip or underskirt are called *suso-yoke*.

Related Garments for Kimono

There are other items needed in order to complete the kimono look. Here are standard items.

半衿 · *han-eri*

長襦袢の衿部分に縫い付ける布。着用する前に、衿に皺がよったりしないように、内側に「衿芯」という芯を入れる。

A strip of cloth sewed onto the collar of *naga-juban*. *Erishin*, a stiffener, is inserted to prevent the collar from wrinkling.

伊達締め · *datejime*

着物の裾を背丈に合わせ、胴を紐で締めておはしょり（13頁）をつくった後、衿の合わせを固定するために結ぶ、着付け用の帯。

An under-sash used to fix both collars of the kimono in place after adjusting the length with *ohashori* tuck (page 13).

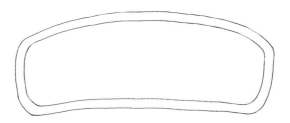

帯板・*obi-ita*

腹側の帯の間に入れる板。帯の形や柄をきれいに見せるために使う。

A plate placed between the front side of layers of obi. It is a stiffener to keep the obi flat.

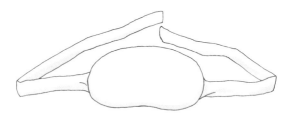

帯枕・*obi-makura*

袋帯や名古屋帯（25頁）を結ぶときに、帯山をつくって固定させるためのもの。帯揚げ（28頁）で包んで用いる。

A small pillow to support and shape the obi knot made with *fukuro-obi* and *nagoya-obi* (page 25). Wrapped with *obi-age* (page 28) when used.

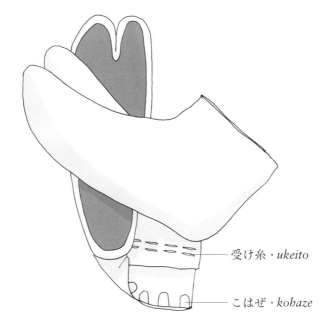

受け糸・*ukeito*

こはぜ・*kohaze*

足袋・*tabi*

和装用の履き物。親指と他の4本の指が分かれた構造になっている。白足袋が正式だが、近年は色柄がついたものも人気。こはぜという金具を受け糸に通して固定する。

Socks for kimono. They divide the big toe for Japanese footwear. While white is the formal color, colored ones have become popular today. Fasten with hooks called *kohaze* and looped strings, *ukeito*.

履き物

和装の履き物は、台(底)に木材を利用する「下駄(げた)」と、木材以外を素材にする「草履(ぞうり)」に大別される。台につけた鼻緒に指をかけて歩く。

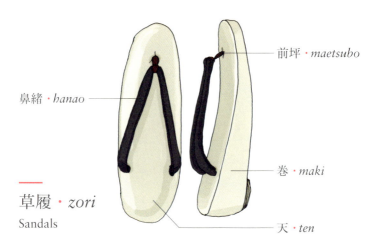

鼻緒・*hanao*
前坪・*maetsubo*
巻・*maki*
天・*ten*

草履・*zori*
Sandals

元は藁(わら)を編んでつくった履物。現在は、コルクの台にエナメルや合成皮革を張ったものが一般的。留袖(16頁)や訪問着(18頁)などの正装には白や淡い色の、高さのある草履が適している。

Originally made of rice straw. Today, it is common to use a cork base and cover it with a plastic material or synthetic leather. White or pale colored *zori* that have a certain height are appropriately worn with formal kimono such as *tomesode* (page 16) and *homongi* (page 18).

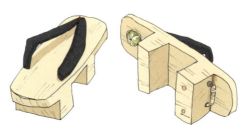

駒下駄・*koma-geta*
Wooden Clogs

二枚歯の下駄のこと。白木と塗りの2種類がある。浴衣の際に素足で履くほか、女性は雨天用の雨下駄として履くことが多い。

Geta with two platforms at the base. There are two types – plain and coated. Worn barefoot with *yukata* as well as with women's kimono on rainy days.

Footwear

Japanese footwear falls roughly into two categories. *Geta* use a wooden base while *zori* use a non-wooden base. Both have thongs called *hanao* to secure one's foot.

のめり・*nomeri* ／千両・*senryo*
Tilted Wooden Clogs

駒下駄の前歯が斜めに切られた形のもの。特に、後ろの歯が駒下駄のようになっているものを「千両」という。のめりの語源は、歩くと前に「のめる」ことから。

A variation of *koma-geta* with an inclined front support. Ones with the same rear support as *komageta* are called *senryo*. The name comes from *nomeru* that means falling forward in Japanese.

雪駄・*setta*
Leather-soled Sandals

竹皮で編んだ台の裏に、革底をじかに貼った男性用の薄い草履。茶人・千利休が考案したものとされる。

Men's *zori* that have a woven bamboo leaf base lined with leather soles. They are believed to have been invented by Sen no Rikyu, the master of tea ceremony.

和装の持ち物

和服を着ている際にふさわしい持ち物を紹介する。また、扇子に関しては単に涼をとるだけではなく、儀式や挨拶の折にも用いられる。

巾着・*kinchaku*
Drawstring Bag

紐で口を開閉するスタイルの布製や皮革製のバッグ。古くは金銭やお守りなど小さなものを入れて用いた。

Made of fabric or leather. People used to carry small objects such as coins and charms in it.

合切袋・*gassai-bukuro*
信玄袋・*shingen-bukuro*
Large Drawstring Bag

財布や携帯品などを入れるのに、程よい大きさの袋。「一切合切(いっさいがっさい)」の持ち物が入ることから名が付いた。籠製の底をつけたものを「籠信玄」という。

A convenient size for carrying a purse and other personal effects. The name comes from *issai-gassai*, which means anything and everything in Japanese. Ones with a basket weave base are called *kago-shingen*.

Accessories

This section introduces adequate accessories for kimono wear. Fans are used not only for cooling off but also at certain rituals and greetings.

風呂敷 · *furoshiki*
Wrapping Cloth

携帯品を包むための、絹、木綿、化繊製の四角い布。江戸時代の風呂屋で、脱いだ衣服を包んだとされることから名が付いた。

A square cloth made of silk, cotton or synthetic material to transport one's personal effects. The name comes from the fact that people used them to bundle their clothes while at public baths, *furo*, in the Edo period.

手拭い · *tenugui*
Handkerchief

薄地の木綿製の布。その名の通り、濡れたり汚れた手を拭うのに用いる。江戸時代には「手拭い被り」といって、被り物としても用いられた。

Japanese hand towels made of thin cotton. People also used them as headscarves in the Edo period.

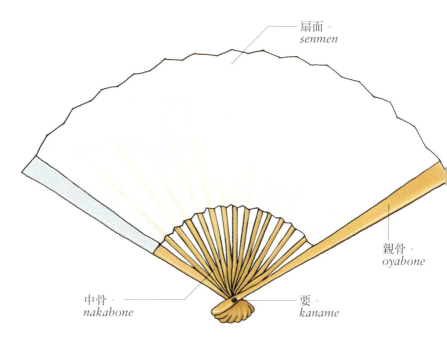

和装の持ち物 — Accessories

夏扇 · *natsu-ogi*
Fan

季節に関係なく涼をとるためにあおぐ扇全般のことをいう。男性用は約22cm、女性用は約20cmが一般的で、扇面は紙や絹でつくられる。

Though *natsu* means summer in Japanese, *natsu-ogi* is the name for fans in general and they are used throughout the year. Usually they are about 9 in. long for men and about 8 in. for women. The surfaces are of paper or silk.

和服

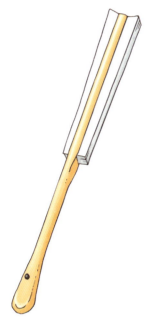

祝儀扇・*shugi-ogi*
白扇・*hakusen*
Celebratory Fan

祝い事や祭事に用いられる扇。男性用は白の地紙に白い竹製の骨でできた白扇(はくせん)、女性用は金銀の地紙に黒の塗り骨が一般的。

Used for celebratory and festive occasions. Usually white paper with a white bamboo frame called *hakusen* for men and gold or silver paper with a black-coated frame for women.

不祝儀扇・*fushugi-ogi*
喪扇・*mosen*
Funeral Fan

葬儀や法事などの不祝儀に用いられる扇。地紙も骨も黒い。

Used for funerals and Buddhist memorial services. Paper and frame are both in black.

茶席扇・*chaseki-ogi* ／茶扇子・*cha-sensu*
Tea Ceremony Fan

茶席で携帯する小ぶりの扇。親骨は白竹と塗りの両方があり、流儀によって定められている。お辞儀や挨拶をするときに膝の前に置くもので、開くことはない。

Smaller fan used at tea ceremonies. Frames can be white bamboo or coated depending on the school. They are placed in front of one's knees when making a bow or greeting and are never opened.

舞扇子・*mai-sensu* ／舞扇・*mai-ogi*
Dance Fan

日本舞踊をはじめとする舞で用いる扇。夏扇より大きく、扇面には美しい柄が描かれている。扇を扱う所作は舞踊の一部になっている。

Used for classical Japanese dance. Larger than *natsu-ogi* and the surface is decorative. The way of handling the fan is incorporated into the dance movements.

茶会の持ち物

着物を着る代表的な機会といえば、茶道における茶会。茶会に必要な持ち物のなかでも代表的なものを紹介する。

帛紗（袱紗）・ *fukusa*
Fukusa Cloth

道具を清めたりするときに使う正絹の布。着物を着て茶席に入るときは、帛紗と懐紙と古帛紗を懐（ふところ）に入れておく。

A silk cloth to cleanse utensils for tea making. When attending a tea ceremony wearing a kimono, one carries a *fukusa* and *kaishi* paper in the bosom of the kimono.

帛紗挟み・ *fukusa-basami*
数寄屋袋・ *sukiya-bukuro*
Bag for *Fukusa* Cloth

茶会に必要な持ち物を入れて携帯するための袋。帛紗などを入れておくことから名が付いた。特に、大振りなものを数寄屋袋という。「数寄屋」とは茶室のことを指す。

Used to transport items for a tea ceremony. The name comes from the fact that most people carry a *fukusa* in the bag. The larger size is called *sukiya-bukuro*. *Sukiya* means tea house or tea room in Japanese.

Items for Tea Ceremony

One of the typical occasions to wear kimono is a tea ceremony. Here are standard items to bring to a tea ceremony.

茶扇子・*cha-sensu*／茶席扇・*chaseki-ogi*
Tea Ceremony Fan

go to page 41.

菓子楊枝と懐紙・*kashiyoji and kaishi*
Pick and Paper Napkin

菓子楊枝とは、茶会でいただく菓子を切るための楊枝のこと。携帯するのはステンレス製が多いが、本来は黒文字楊枝を使用する。懐紙とは、菓子をのせるための二つ折りの和紙の束。昔はいろいろな用途があった。

A pick is used to cut Japanese confectionaries served at a tea ceremony. *Kaishi* is a bundle of folded *washi* papers on which you place the confectionaries. *Kaishi* paper was used for various purposes in the past.

色の名前

日本には、花鳥風月や染料に由来する色の名前が豊富にある。微妙な色合いの違いを見分けて名前をつけた先人の感性が反映されている。そのごく一部を、古くから伝わる染め方を交えて紹介する。

洗朱・*araishu*

薄い朱色。朱色の布を洗ったあとの少し色が抜けたイメージ。

Pale vermilion. The color of vermilion fabric after being washed and slightly worn.

紅色・*kurenai-iro (beni-iro)*

少し紫がかった赤色。「紅」は紅花（べにばな）の色素でつくられた化粧料。

Slightly purple-ish red. *Kurenai* is a makeup made of natural red pigment derived from safflower.

唐紅色（韓紅色）・*kara-kurenai-iro*

紅色より黄みを帯びた色。中国伝来の紅花で繰り返し染めた濃い紅色。

A yellow-tinted *kurenai-iro*, which is a dark red dyed repeatedly with safflower native to China.

Japanese Colors

In Japan, there are many colors named after the seasonal beauties of nature or various dye compounds. They reflect the sensitivity of the people of the past who were able to distinguish subtle differences in colors. Here are a small number of the many examples that exist.

臙脂色・*enji-iro*

少し黒味がかった濃い赤色。「臙脂」は、コチニールという虫からとった顔料で染める。

Dark red with a tint of black. Dyed in pigment derived from the cochineal insect.

黄丹・*oni*

黄色と丹（赤色）が混ざったオレンジ系色。古来、黄丹の衣は皇太子の礼服だった。

A kind of orange with a mixture of yellow and red. *Oni* kimono were formal wear for princes in ancient time.

弁柄色・*bengara-iro*

明るい茶系色。「弁柄」は、酸化鉄を主成分とする顔料。インド・ベンガル地方が産出地であることから名が付いた。

Light brown. *Bengara* is a pigment consisting mainly of iron oxide. The name comes from the fact that the pigment is produced in Bengal in India.

香色・*ko-iro*

ベージュに似た薄茶色。香りのよい丁子（ちょうじ）の木を煎じた汁で染める。

Pale brown similar to beige. Dyed in infused aromatic cloves.

山吹色・*yamabuki-iro*

ややオレンジがかった黄色。春に咲く山吹の花の色から名が付いた。

Slightly orange-ish yellow. Named after the color of the flower of Japanese kerria that blooms in spring.

鶯色・*uguisu-iro*

やや黒茶が混ざった緑色。鶯の羽の色から名が付いた。

Green with a tint of brown and gray. Refers to the color of the wings of a Japanese Nightingale.

萌葱（萌黄）色・
moegi-iro

明るい緑色。萌え出る葱の芽の色から名が付いた。

Light green. From the color of budding leek sprouts.

若竹色・
wakatake-iro

春に伸びる若い竹の幹のような爽やかな緑色。日本の色名には、基本の色より明るく新鮮に見える色に「若」とつけることがよくある。

A fresh green suggesting young bamboo trunks in the spring. Names for the colors that are lighter than the original basic colors often include "*waka*," meaning young in Japanese.

浅葱色・*asagi-iro*

緑色を帯びた、あざやかな青色。薄い（浅い）葱の色という意味で名が付いた。

Bright blue with a tint of green. Named after the color of leeks. "*Asa*" means pale or light in Japanese.

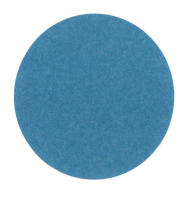

藍色・*ai-iro*

濃く暗い青色。タデアイという植物からつくる「藍」で染めた色には、さまざまな色合いと色名がある。

Deep blue. Dyed with indigo, the color has many variations in the hue and in name.

縹（花田）色・*hanada-iro*

ややくすんだ藍色。純粋に藍だけで染められる。濃淡によって「濃縹（こきはなだ）」、「浅縹（うすきはなだ）」などと呼び分けられる。

A slightly dull version of *ai-iro*. Dyed only with natural indigo. The darker hue is called *koki-hanada* while the paler hue is called *usuki-hanada*.

藤色・*fuji-iro*

淡い紫色。藤の花の色から名が付いた。

Pale purple. Named after the color of wisteria flowers.

江戸紫・*edo-murasaki*

濃い赤紫色。武蔵野に自生する紫草の根を用いて、江戸で染めたことから名が付いた。

Burgundy. The name comes from the fact people in Edo, today's Tokyo, started to dye fabric with the root of the purple gromwell, which grew wildly in the area.

利休鼠・*rikyu-nezumi*

やや緑がかった灰色。侘びさびを連想させる色で、茶人・千利休の名が付いている。

A slightly greenish gray. Associated with the concept of *wabi-sabi*, it is named after the tea master – Sen no Rikyu.

鈍色・*nibi-iro*

薄墨色。平安時代以降の喪服には、この色が用いられた。

Dark gray. Used for mourning dress after the Heian period.

伝統的な文様

染織をはじめとする日本の工芸品には、さまざまな文様が表されている。ここではよく目にする文様とその名前を紹介する。

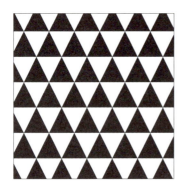

鱗・*uroko*
Scale

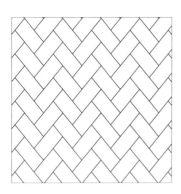

檜垣・*higaki*
Cypress Fence

網代・*ajiro*
Wicker

Traditional Patterns

Various types of patterns are used for Japanese crafts, including textiles. Here are typical examples.

亀甲・*kikko*
Hexagon

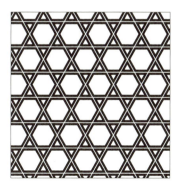

籠目・*kagome*
Reticulum

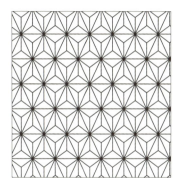

麻の葉・*asanoha*
Flax Leaf

紗綾形・*sayagata*
Modified Fylfot

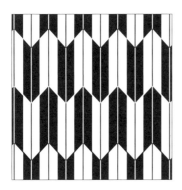

矢羽根・*yabane*
Arrow Feathers

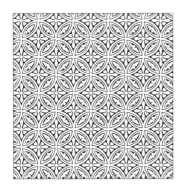

七宝繋ぎ・
shippo-tsunagi
Gem Repetition

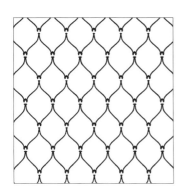

立涌・*tatewaku*
Vapor

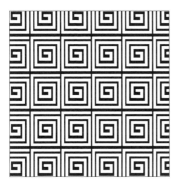

雷・*rai*
Spiral

青海波・*seigaiha*
Wave

縞模様

一見、単純で同じように見える縞にも、それぞれ特徴を捉えた名前がある。ここでは一部を紹介する。

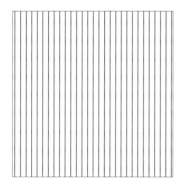

千筋・*sen-suji*
Thousand Stripe

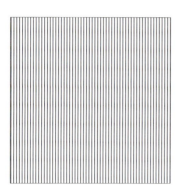

万筋・*man-suji*
Ten Thousand Stripe

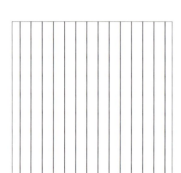

大名筋・*daimyo-suji*
Thin Vertical Stripe

Stripes

Despite their similarities, there are specific names for each strip pattern. Here are typical examples.

棒縞・*bo-jima*
Bar Stripe

矢鱈縞・*yatara-jima*
Random Stripe

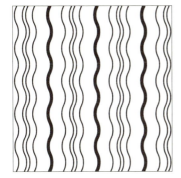

よろけ縞・*yoroke-jima*
Wavy Stripe

格子模様

縞模様（54頁）と同様に、単純そうに見える格子模様にもさまざまな名前がある。ここではその一部を紹介する。

市松模様
ichimatsu-moyo

Checkered Pattern

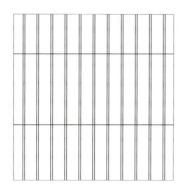

障子格子
shoji-goshi

Shoji Grid

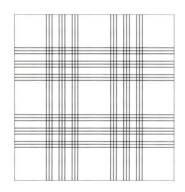

三筋格子
misuji-goshi

Three Line Grid

Grids

As with stripes (page 54), there are specific names for each grid pattern. Here are typical examples.

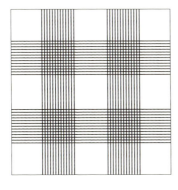

弁慶格子・*benke-goshi*

Benke Gingham

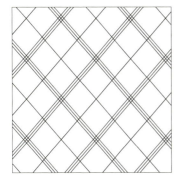

業平格子・*narihira-goshi*

Diagonal Grid

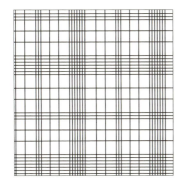

翁格子・*okina-goshi*

Okina Plaid

家紋

家紋とは、家々が古くから定めている紋のこと。紋付きの着物は礼装となり、紋の数が増えるに従って格が上がる。ここでは、膨大にある家紋の一部を紹介する。

五三ノ桐 · *gosan no kiri*
Five and Three Paulownia

蔦 · *tsuta*
Ivy

桔梗 · *kikyo*
Balloon Flower

Family Crests

Family crests have been used to identify families for centuries. Kimono which display family crests are formal wear and the number of crests defines the rank of the kimono.

揚羽蝶 · *agehacho*

Swallowtail Butterfly

丸に剣片喰 · *maru-ni-kenkatabami*

Sorrel and Sword in Circle

丸に九枚笹 · *maru-ni-kumaizasa*

Nine Bamboo Leaves in Circle

丸に隅立四ツ目 ·
maru-ni-sumitate-yotsume

Four Squares in Circle

丸に三ツ柏 ·
maru-ni-mitsugashiwa

Three Oak Leaves in Circle

丸に橘 ·
maru-ni-tachibana

Mandarin Orange in Circle

丸に違い鷹羽
maru-ni-chigai-takanoha

Two Feathers Crossing in Circle

丸に梅鉢
maru-ni-umebachi

Plum Blossoms in Circle

丸に横木瓜
maru-ni-yoko-mokko

Japanese Quince in Circle

婚礼の装束

神前式など日本に古くから伝わる婚礼では、特別な着物を身に着ける。特に「白無垢」は花嫁にとって特別な衣装。挙式では白無垢を、披露宴では色打掛を着る人が多い。

角隠し・*tsunokakushi*
Headwear
→ p. 130

筥迫・*hakoseko*
Purse
→ p. 141

白無垢・*shiromuku*

White Kimono

打掛・掛下・帯から小物類まで、白一色に統一した和装のこと。婚礼で着る際は、花嫁の身の清らかさと、どんな色（嫁ぎ先の習わし）にも染まることを意味している。

A style of kimono in which every item is white, including *uchikake*, *kakeshita*, obi and accessories. When worn at a wedding, white symbolizes the purity of the bride and how she is going to adopt a new color, the custom of the family she is marrying into.

Wedding Attire

Special kimono are worn for Japanese wedding ceremonies. *Shiromuku* for brides is particular. Many people wear *shiromuku* at the ceremony and *iro-uchikake* robes for reception banquets.

1

打掛 · *uchikake*

Robe

着物の上から羽織り、帯を締めずに裾を引く長着。室町時代以降、打掛は武家の女性の礼装だった。

Worn like a coat without an obi, it was formal wear for women of samurai families after the Muromachi period.

2

掛下 · *kakeshita*

Under Robe Kimono

打掛の下に着る着物のこと。

Worn under *uchikake*.

3

文金高島田 · *bunkin-taka-shimada*

Coiffure for Bride

正装の花嫁が結う日本髪の一種。江戸時代には武家の未婚の女性や遊女の一部に結われていた。

A style of Japanese coiffure for brides worn with formal attire. This style was popular among unmarried women from samurai families and prostitutes in the Edo period.

4

末広 · *suehiro*

Celebratory Fan

祝儀用の扇子のことを、「（扇のように）末広がりに幸せになるように」という願いを込めて「末広」という。

Fans used at celebratory occasions. *Suehiro* means open end in Japanese, implying everlasting happiness.

白扇・*hakusen*
→ p. 40

足袋・*tabi*
→ p. 33

草履・*zori*
→ p. 34

紋付羽織袴・*montsuki-haori-hakama*

Formal Kimono for Men

現代における男性の和装の第一礼装。江戸時代は下級武士の装いだった。それが庶民の礼装として着用されるようになり、明治時代に五つ紋付きの黒無地長着と羽織、袴の組み合わせが礼装として採用された。

This is the most formal men's kimono today. Worn by low-ranking samurai in the Edo period, it became popular as formal wear among ordinary people. Five family crests on a set of black kimono and a *haori* coat worn with a *hakama* skirt became the official formal wear in the Meiji period.

1

紋・*mon*
Family Crest

礼装の着物には家紋を入れる。入れる数には一、三、五があり、数が多いほど格が上がる。一つ紋は背中の衿下に、三つ紋は背中と両袖の後ろ、五つ紋は背中・両袖・両胸と決まっている。

Formal kimono have a family crest. The number of crests could be one, three or five and the higher in number, the more formal. One crest is placed in the back and below the collar. In the case of three, there are two additional crests behind the sleeves. In the case of five, another two are found on both sides of the chest.

2

羽織・*haori*
Short Coat

長着（着物）の上に着る丈の短い外衣。衿を外側に折って着る。女性用の羽織もあり、正装向きのものからカジュアルなものまで種類がある。

Worn over kimono. The collar is folded over when worn. Women wear *haori* as well and there are a variety from formal to casual.

3

羽織紐（白房付き）・
haori-himo (shirofusa-tsuki)
Strings with White Tassel

白房のついた組紐。羽織の胸元につけられた小さい金具（「ちち」という）に両端を掛ける。

Hooked onto small loops on *haori* called *chichi*.

4

馬乗袴・*umanori-bakama*
Divided Skirt

下半身につける衣服を「袴」といい、腰の位置で紐を結んで留める。二股に分かれているものを馬乗袴、分かれていないものを「行灯（あんどん）袴」という。「仙台平」と呼ばれる絹織物が正式。

Hakama are worn over the kimono and tied at the waist. Divided *hakama*, similar to trousers, are called *umanori-bakama* (horse-riding *hakama*) and undivided skirts are called *andon-bakama* (lantern *hakama*). The formal material is a silk fabric called *sendai-hira*.

社寺の装束

神道や仏教に携わる人々には、定められた装束がある。ここではその一部を紹介するが、階位や宗派などによって装束に差異が見られる。

僧侶の装束
Buddhist Priests

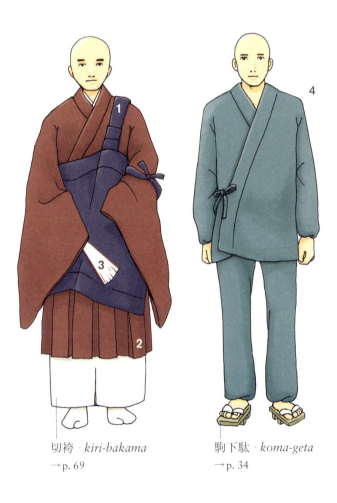

切袴・*kiri-bakama*
→ p. 69

駒下駄・*koma-geta*
→ p. 34

Priest Attire

People working for Shinto shrines and Buddhist temples wear certain kimono. Details may differ depending on one's class and school.

1

袈裟・*kesa*

Monk's Stole

僧侶が左肩から掛けて衣を覆う法衣。元々は大小問わない不要な布を縫い合わせてつくられた。宗派によってさまざまな色味があるが、いずれも濁色になっている。その色を表すサンスクリット語kasayaが語源となっている。

A clerical garment worn over a monk's left shoulder. Originally made of leftover fabrics in different sizes patched together. Color varies depending on the school, though they are always found in murky tones. The name comes from *kasaya*, which means brown or saffron dye in Sanskrit.

2

直綴・*jikitotsu*

Monk's Robe

上衣と下衣を綴り合わせた僧侶の衣服で、腰から下の部分に襞（ひだ）がついている。

Upper garment and *hakama* are sewed together. The bottom half is pleated.

3

中啓・*chukei*

Open Celebratory Fan

畳んだ状態でも、少し先が啓（ひら）いた扇のこと。儀式の際に持ち、威儀を正すためのもの。室町時代に、正装の際に用いられたとされる。

The tip is slightly open even when closed. An instrument to hold during Buddhist rituals. It was a formal wear accessary in the Muromachi period.

4

作務衣・*samue*

Monk's Work Clothes

僧侶の作業着。上は筒袖、下はズボン状になっている。

Characterized by tight-sleeves and trousers.

神職の常装 — Shinto Priests   巫女の装束 — *Miko*, Shrine Maidens

狩衣 · *kariginu*

Kariginu Ceremonial Kimono

肩部分に切れ込みが入った、動きやすさを重視した上衣。平安時代に鷹狩り用の服として、上流階級が使ったのが始まり。かつては、必要に応じて袖括りの紐を絞っていた。

With the wearer's mobility in mind, this upper garment has slits on the shoulders. It used to be hunting wear for the nobles in the Heian period.

烏帽子 · *eboshi*

Headgear

神事の際に被り、威儀を正すための帽子。平安時代では、朝廷に仕える人々の日常的な被り物だった。

Worn at shrine rituals today to uphold the dignity of the event. In the Heian period, people working for the Imperial court would wear it on a daily basis.

3

差袴・*sashiko*／切袴・*kiri-bakama*
Divided Skirt for Shinto Priest

腰につける袴には、後ろに引くほど裾の長い「長袴」（119頁）と、足首までの長さの「切袴」がある。神職がつける切袴は差袴とも呼ばれ、階級によって色と文様が異なる。無紋の浅葱色（47頁）は若い神職用。

Hakama with a long train are called *naga-bakama* (page 119), whereas, the ankle-length version is called *kiri-bakama*. *Kiri-bakama* worn by Shinto priests are called *sashiko* and they vary in color and pattern depending on the wearers rank. Plain *asagi-iro* (page 47) is worn by young priests.

4

笏・*shaku*
Wooden Mace

神事の際に持ち、威儀を正すための道具。古代中国において、役人が皇帝の命令をメモ書きするために使用されたという。

An instrument to hold during Shinto rituals. It was used to take notes of the emperors' orders in ancient China.

5

緋袴・*hi-bakama*
Scarlet Divided Skirt

現在では巫女の装束としてよく目にする緋色の切袴。平安時代においては、宮廷の女性たちが着用するものだった。

Worn by shrine maidens today. It was court attire for women in the Heian period.

6

上指糸・*uwasashi-ito*
Decorative Thread

緋袴の腰部分に施された装飾のこと。糸とはいうものの、実際は紐ほどの太さがある。

An ornament sewed on the waist of *hi-bakama*. Though called a thread, it is indeed as thick as a string.

7

白衣・*hakue (byakue/shirokinu)*

身の丈と同じ長さで仕立てた純白の着物。

Ankle length white kimono.

伝統行事の装束

日本の伝統行事にはそれぞれに適した装束がある。ここでは現在でもよく目にする祭りの装束と、日本の国技である相撲に関わる装束を紹介する。

力士の装束
Sumo Wrestlers

行司の装束
Sumo Referees

1
化粧回し・*keshomawashi*
Ceremonial Loincloth

回しは腰にまとう布（ふんどし）の意で、相撲の力士などがつける。関取（十両以上の力士）が土俵入りの際に締める儀式用の回しを化粧回しといい、力士に応じてさまざまな刺繍が施されている。

Mawashi is the loincloth worn by sumo wrestlers. *Keshomawashi* is worn by ranked wrestlers when performing the ring entering ceremony. Each wrestler has own distinguishing embroidery on it.

Attire for Traditional Events

There is a particular garment worn at each Japanese traditional event. This section introduces attires for festivals and sumo wrestling.

2

直垂・*hitatare*

Hitatare Caremonial Kimono

胸元に綴じ紐のついた着物。元々は平安時代の武士の日常着だった。江戸時代以降に見直され、公家や大名の礼装となる。現在の行司の装束は鎌倉時代に鎧（よろい）の下に着た「鎧直垂」風。「垂領（たりくび）」という、今日でも見られる衿の形から名が付いたとされる。

A variation of kimono with tied threads on the chest. What was once everyday attire for samurai in the Heian period became formal wear for court nobles and feudal lords in the Edo period. The ones sumo referees wear today are based on the type worn under armor in the Kamakura period.

3

侍烏帽子・*samurai-eboshi*

Samurai Headgear

烏帽子には立烏帽子、風折烏帽子、侍烏帽子など多種あるが、行司装束には鎌倉時代の武士が直垂に合わせて用いた侍烏帽子が使われている。

There are various kinds of *eboshi* headgear. Sumo referees wear *samurai-eboshi* that was worn by samurai in the Kamakura period together with *hitatare*.

4

軍配団扇・*gunbai-uchiwa*

Referee's Fan

審判動作に使うのが軍配団扇。戦国時代の武将たちが使っていたものと同様の形をしている。書かれている文字や模様は行司の好みによる。欅（けやき）や黒檀（こくたん）などの堅木製。

Used by sumo referees to indicate the victor. It is the same shape as those used by samurai from the Sengoku period. Each referee customizes the writing and design of his fan. Made of hardwood, such as Japanese zelkova, and ebony.

祭り衣装
Festival Attire

1

鉢巻・*hachimaki*
Headband

頭の上部（鉢）に巻く手拭い（37頁）。気合を入れる意味合いがある。

Tenugui (page 37) wrapped around the upper part of the head. Worn as a symbol of concentration.

2

袢纏・*hanten*
Casual Short Coat

羽織を簡略にした丈の短い上衣。祭りでは、背や衿に家紋を染めた「印（しるし）袢纏」を着る。昔は仕事着・防寒着として広く用いられていた。

A simplified short version of *haori*. *Shirushi-hanten* with a family crest dyed on the back or collar is worn at festivals. People used to wear them as work clothes and winter jackets.

3

地下足袋・*jika-tabi*
Rubber-soled Socks

ゴム底の付いた足袋（33頁）のことで、履き物なしでじかに歩くことができる。主に戸外で労働作業をする人が履く。

A type of footwear modeled on *tabi* socks (page 33). Often worn by workmen who work outdoor.

4

草鞋・*waraji*
Straw Sandals

草履（34頁）に形が似た、藁（わら）で編まれた履き物。足に括り付ける紐がついているので、激しい動きをしても脱げない。

Similar in shape to *zori* (page 34), they are made from woven rice straw. Attached ropes secure feet to the base despite strenuous movement.

5

腹掛け・*haragake*
Apron

胸から腹までを覆って、背中で共布を結ぶ衣服。祭り以外では、職人などが着る作業着でもあった。古くは幼児が寝冷えしないように着せていたものも「腹掛け」と呼んだ。

Covering the chest and belly, it's tied in the back. Aside from festivals, once worn by craftsmen as work clothes.

6

股引・*momohiki*
Trousers

洋服のズボンに似た衣服。祭り以外では、職人などが着る作業着である。江戸時代には男性の普段着だった。現在では股引の形が変化して、「ズボン下」「ステテコ」と呼ばれる男性用の下着になっている。

Aside from festivals, worn by craftsmen as work clothes. They were everyday attire for men in the Edo period. Today, variations called *zubon-shita* or *suteteko* are worn as a kind of long underwear.

日本の時代区分
Japanese Time Periods

和服や古くから伝わる日本の装束は、時代によって変遷しつづけてきた。ここでは、本書によく登場する時代を紹介するが、各時代区分の始期・終期に関しては諸説ある。

Japanese traditional clothing has evolved through different historical periods. Here is the list of the time periods that frequently appear in this book. The beginning and the end of each era are approximations.

794-1185 平安時代　Heian Period

京都に平安京がつくられてから約400年間を指す。天皇と、それに仕える公卿が政治的権力を持った。文学をはじめとして、雅な文化が進歩した。

The period when the capital was located in Heian-kyo, today's Kyoto. The emperor and the very few most powerful people attached to the court held political power. An elegant and sophisticated culture flourished, literature being a particularly notable example.

1185-1333 鎌倉時代　Kamakura Period

鎌倉に幕府が置かれた武家政権の時代を指す。源氏の将軍が3代つづいたあとは、実権が北条氏に移り、後醍醐天皇率いる反対勢力により滅亡。

A samurai regime at a time when the federal government was located in Kamakura. After three generations of Shogun from the Genji family, the Hojos took power. Opposition led by the Emperor Godaigo ended the era.

1336-1573 室町時代　Muromachi Period

京都室町に足利家による幕府が置かれた時代を指す。15代将軍までつづいたが、後半は各地の大名が天下統一をめざして争う「戦国時代」となった。

The Ashikaga family took power and re-located the government to Muromachi, Kyoto. This lasted for 15 generations with the late years dissolving into civil war. Feudal lords from throughout Japan were fighting each other for power.

1573-1603 安土桃山時代(織豊時代) Azuchi-Momoyama Period

織田信長と豊臣秀吉が政権を掌握した時代を指す。信長の死後、秀吉が天下統一を果たすものの、関ヶ原の戦いで徳川家康に敗れ終焉を迎える。

The period in which Oda Nobunaga and Toyotomi Hideyoshi were in power. After the death of Nobunaga, Hideyoshi came to govern the nation, but lost the battle with Tokugawa Ieyasu at Sekigahara.

1603-1867 江戸時代　Edo Period

江戸（東京）に徳川家による幕府が置かれた260年間を指す。武士が支配する身分制社会で、あらゆる制度や設備が整えられた。鎖国外交を展開するなかで、江戸文化が花開いた。

The 260 year period when the Tokugawa family governed the nation from Edo, present-day Tokyo. It was a time in which many social systems and infrastructure were developed. Social stratification was characterized by class in a hierarchy in which samurai were eminent. Under the seclusion policy, which sealed Japan off from the outside world, the period saw a rich and distinctive culture develop.

1867-1912 明治時代　Meiji Period

明治天皇の治世の時代を指す。江戸幕府が朝廷に政権を返上したことで、天皇制の中央集権的な国家へ転換した。西洋文化が盛んに取り入れられた。

This period corresponded with the reign of Emperor Meiji. After the Edo government returned power to the Imperial court, Japanese society moved to centralization under the Imperial system. Cultural development was greatly influenced by the West.

伝統芸能

JAPANESE TRADITIONAL PERFORMING ARTS

能装束

能楽は室町時代に大成された歌舞劇。謡（うたい）、囃子（はやし）、舞以外にも注目すべきは衣装。役柄に応じて衣装を組み合わせて着付ける。ここでは典型的な出立（いでたち）を紹介する。

女性の出立 —『熊野』熊野
Female Costume – Yuya in "Yuya"

面・*omote*
Mask
→ p. 84

中啓・*chukei*
Open Celebratory Fan
→ p. 67

Noh Costumes

Noh is a form of Japanese musical drama developed during the Muromachi period. Aside from the enticing music and dance performance, its costumes are particularly notable. Actors wear various types of costumes in different combinations depending on the characters they play. Here are the four typical types of costumes.

1

唐織・*karaori*

主に女性や若い青年貴族の役が着る着物。草花や流水など自然を表した模様が多い。立体的に見える浮織が特徴。赤い色が入った唐織は若い女性、赤い色が入らないものは中年以降の女性であることを表している。

A kimono mainly worn by young females or young aristocrats. It usually has motifs from nature such as plants, flowers and streams of water. Characterized by embossed brocade called *ukiori*, this style with red indicates a young woman, and without red an older woman.

2

摺箔・*surihaku*

布地に金銀の箔を貼り付け、文様を表した着物。内着として着るので通常は衿元しか見えないが、鬼女の役などでは内着の上半身をあらわにして尋常でない様子を表現する。

Decorated with gold and silver leaves, this kimono is usually worn underneath the kimono with only the collar visible to the audience. However, some characters, such as female demons expose the upper half of the kimono in an expression of the uncanny.

3

鬘帯・*kazura-obi*

鬘を留めるための鉢巻状の布。後ろで結んで、長く垂らしている。女役ではほとんどの役に用いられ、さまざまな柄がある。

A strip of cloth used as a headband for female characters. Tied in the back with the rest hanging down. There are various colors and patterns.

舞の出立―『井筒』杜若の精
Dance Costume – Spirit of Iris in "Izutsu"

摺箔・*surihaku*
→ p 77

1
長絹・*choken*

代表的な広袖の表着。紗(しゃ)や絽(ろ)など薄い生地に、金銀の糸で文様を施したものが多い。胸元と袖に「露(つゆ)」と呼ばれる紐飾りがついている。

Noh's signature wide-sleeve robe. Usually made of a thin material, such as silk gauze, accompanied by gold and silver thread patterns. It has decorative strings called *tsuyu* on the chest and sleeves.

2
縫箔・*nuihaku*

刺繍や箔で文様を表した着物。両袖を脱いで、袖を腰に巻きつける「腰巻」スタイルにすることが多い。

An array of embroidery and leaf patterns, this kimono usually is worn with the sleeves wrapped around the waist.

3
胸紐・*munehimo*

胸元に垂らしてある、房付きの紐。袖紐と同色で、着用するたびにつけ替える。

Replaceable tasseled string hung on the chest. Same color as the string on the *choken* sleeves.

4
菊綴・*kikutoji*

袖の中心にある結び目状の紐。二枚の布の継ぎ目を補強するためのものだったが、やがて飾りになった。

Strings tied along the top of the sleeves. Originally reinforcing the seams on the sleeves, it evolved into an ornament over time.

能装束 Noh Costumes

伝統芸能

武将の出立 ー『屋島』源義経

Samurai Costume – Minamoto Yoshitsune in "Yashima"

1

法被 · *happi*

和服の上着の一種。イラストは法被のなかでも、金襴で豪快な意匠を織り出した、能装束特有のもの。裏地のついた袷（あわせ）の法被は、武将や鬼神、天狗などの荒々しい役を表す。前身頃（まえみごろ）と後ろ身頃が離れており、裾のところにある共布「合引（あいびき）」で繋げる。

A type of Japanese coat. Here is the special Noh costume version with a glorious design. Lined *happi* indicate brutal characters such as warlords, demons or *tengu* goblins.

2

厚板 · *atsuita*

主に男性や鬼神などの役が着る着物。赤い色が入った厚板は、若年の男子であることを表す。

A kimono mainly worn by male and demon characters. In red, it implies youth.

3

半切 · *hangire (hangiri)*

足首までの長さの、大きなひだがある袴。長袴（119頁）に対して、裾を切った袴の意。金襴でさまざまな模様を表したものが多い。

Ankle length *hakama* with large pleats. The name means a cut-off of *naga-bakama* (page 119). It usually has flaring expressive patterns.

4

腰帯 · *koshi-obi*

細長い布帯。腰の後ろ部分と前に垂れる部分に薄い板が縫い込まれているため、締めたときに美しい形になる。

A strip of fabric used as obi. Thin boards are sewn onto the back and front droops to keep shape when worn.

5

梨子打烏帽子 · *nashiuchi-eboshi*

兜の下に着用するやわらかい被り物のこと。烏帽子にはいろいろな種類がある。

Soft headgear worn under *kabuto* helmet. There are various types of *eboshi* headgear.

能装束

Noh Costumes

伝統芸能

老人の出立 －『恋重荷』山科荘司
Old Man Costume – Yamashina Shoji in "Koi-no-Omoni"

厚板・*atsuita*
→ p. 81

中啓・*chukei*
Open Celebratory Fan
→ p. 67

腰帯・*koshi-obi*
→ p 81

1

水衣・*mizugoromo*

一般庶民の役が着る広袖形の着物。無地のものを「絓（しけ）水衣」、横糸が波状になったものを「縷（よれ）水衣」という。縷水衣は身分の低い役に用いられる。

A wide-sleeved kimono for ordinary people. With a single colored fabric, they are called *shike-mizugoromo* and those with a wavy weft, which are worn by people of low birth, are called *yore-mizugoromo*.

2

尉髪・*jogami*

能に登場する老人の髪型の一種。鬘は馬尾毛（ばす）といって、馬の尾の毛でできている。鬘をつける際、そのつど毛を結い上げ、元結（129頁）をかける。

A hairstyle for old Noh characters. The wig is made of horsetail. Hairs on the wig are tied by hand with *mottoi* strings (page 129) each time.

能面

能で用いられる面のことを、能面もしくは面（おもて）という。表情に乏しいように見えるが、面の向きを変えることで喜怒哀楽を表す。老若男女さまざまな面があるが、その一部を紹介する。

小面・*ko-omote*

最も年若い、処女の役につける女面。純真さが表れている。小面よりやや年上の役には「若女（わかおんな）」をつける。

Mask for a very young woman and a virgin. It carries a sense of innocence. A slightly older character wears *waka-onna*.

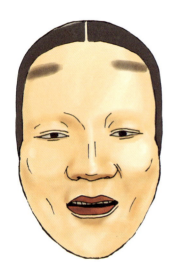

深井・*fukai*

中年女性の役につける女面。特に、悲劇の母親役でつけられることが多い。哀愁をたたえた表情をしている。

Mask for a middle age woman. Often used for a tragic mother, it carries a sense of grief.

Noh Masks

Masks used in Noh performances are called *omote*. Depending upon the angle from which they are seen, a seemingly vacant mask can express a variety of emotions. There are many types of Noh masks for characters ranging from young to old. Here are some examples.

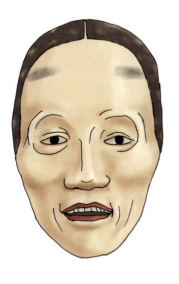

痩女・*yase-onna*

地獄で妄執に苦しむ、痩せ衰えた幽霊などの役につける面。

Mask for a weary ghost or someone who suffers in hell.

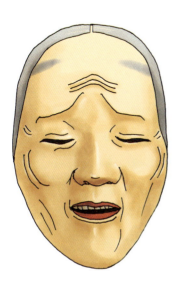

姥・*uba*

気品のある老婆の役につける面。

Mask for an elegant old woman.

翁・*okina*
白式尉・*hakushikijo*

満面の笑みを浮かべた老人の面。幸福をもたらす祝福の面として、尊ばれている。この面が使われる曲目『翁』は特別な能で、めでたいハレの日に上演される。白式尉に対して、黒式尉もある。

A mask with the big grin of an old man. It is regarded as a celebratory mask that brings happiness. A Noh repertoire called "Okina," in which this mask appears, is performed on celebratory occasions.

般若・*hannya*

激しい嫉妬のあまり鬼と化し、角が生えた女性の面。怨恨と悲壮が表情に込められている。

A horned mask for a woman who has turned into a demon out of violent jealousy. It carries a sense of resentment and desperation.

飛出・*tobide*

大きな目が飛び出た鬼神の面。鬼神とは、超人的な力を持つ存在のことで、人間の死後の霊や化け物を指す。

A mask of a demon in which the eyes are popping out. Demons in Noh have superhuman strength and suggest the spirit of the afterlife or of a monster.

大癋見・*obeshimi*

天狗の役につける面。「へしむ」とは、口を閉じて強く力んで、相手を威嚇（いかく）すること。「小癋見」という面は閻魔（えんま）大王や鬼神の役につける。

Mask for a *tengu* goblin. In Japanese, *heshimu* means to intimidate someone by pursing one's lips in a frown. A *kobeshimi* mask is worn by a god of death or a demon.

能舞台

能舞台は元々、野外にあったため、屋内にあっても屋根と柱がついている。能役者だけでなく、音楽を演奏する「囃子方(はやしかた)」と、バックコーラスの「地謡(じうたい)」が舞台に上がる。

1
本舞台・*hombutai*
Main Stage

約6m四方の総檜(ひのき)張りの舞台。床板は縦張りで、光るほどに磨きこまれている。足拍子で響きの良い音を出すため、舞台の下に甕(かめ)が埋められていることがある。

About 6m square cypress floor. The floorboards are installed lengthwise and the stage floor is very well polished. Sometime large jars are buried under the stage so that the actors' footsteps will resonate more powerfully.

2
階・*kizahashi*
Stairs

舞台正面につけられた階段。昔は、役者が客席の貴人から褒美をいただくときに使っていたが、現在は通常使われることがない。

Located at the center of the stage's front edge. Actors used to use these steps to receive gifts from officials in the audience. It is not commonly used today.

Noh Stage

Since Noh used to be performed outdoors, the modern indoor stage still retains the roof and pillars of its predecessor. Musicians and chorus members are also seated on the stage.

橋掛り・*hashigakari*
Corridor

揚幕（93頁）から本舞台へとつづく通路のこと。登場人物や囃子方が入退場をする渡り廊下で、ここでも演技が行われる。この世とあの世をつなぐ道とされる。

Connecting the *agemaku* (page 93) and the main stage, actors and musicians enter the stage from here. Sometimes performances take place along the corridor. It is regarded as the path that divides the land of the living from the afterlife.

見所・*kensho*
Audience Seats

客席のこと。本舞台の真正面の席を「正面」、本舞台を真横から見る席を「脇正面」、正面と脇正面の間にある扇形のエリアを「中正面」という。

Divided into three areas.

Shomen: facing the stage.
Waki-shomen: viewing the stage from the side.
Naka-shomen: a fan-shaped area between the two.

本舞台
Main Stage

1

鏡板・*kagami-ita*

Back Wall

松が描かれた舞台正面の羽目板。松であることについては、常緑で特定の季節を象徴しない、門松のように神を迎えて芸を奉納する意味が込められている、など諸説ある。音響効果もある。

Decorated with a painting of a pine tree. There are different stories about the origin of pine tree. Some say since they are evergreen, they don't represent any specific season. Other may say it is to welcome spirits like a *kadomatsu* in order to dedicate the performance. The wall also has an amplifying acoustic effect.

2

シテ柱・*shite-bashira*

Shite Pillar

シテが立つ位置に近い柱。シテとは主役のこと。その曲目の前後半で、シテの姿が変わるとき、「前シテ」「後（のち）シテ」と呼び分けられる。

Closest pillar to the position of the *shite*, the central character.

3

ワキ柱・*waki-bashira*

Waki Pillar

ワキが座る位置に近い柱。ワキとは脇役のことで、物語の進行役を務める。たいてい最初に出てきて、自己紹介や説明をしたあと、ワキ柱のそばにずっと座っている。

Closest pillar to the seating of the *waki*, a secondary character who usually appears on stage first and tells the audience where and when the story is unfolding. He stays seated by the *waki* pillar after that.

4

目付柱・*metsuke-bashira*

Sighting Pillar

演能中の能役者の目印になる柱。面をつけると視野が狭くなるため、目付柱を頼りに歩みを進めたり、舞ったりする。

It plays an important role in assisting actors who are wearing masks to orient themselves on the stage.

5

笛柱・*fue-bashira*

Musicians' Pillar

囃子方の笛が座る位置に近い柱。

Closest pillar to the flute player.

能舞台 ┃ Noh Stage

伝統芸能

橋掛り
Corridor

___1

一の松・*ichi no matsu*
First Pine Tree

___2

二の松・*ni no matsu*
Second Pine Tree

___3

三の松・*san no matsu*
Third Pine Tree

―― 4

揚幕（能）・*agemaku*
Noh Curtain

能役者と囃子方（94頁）の出入り口。出入りする際に、内側から2本の竹で幕を上に揚げる。

Entrance for actors and musicians (page 94). The curtain is raised with two bamboo sticks from inside as they enter.

1

囃子方・*hayashikata*

Musicians

笛、小鼓（こつづみ）、大鼓（おおつづみ）、太鼓を演奏する人々のこと。揚幕（93頁）から登場する。演目によっては太鼓が入らない場合もある。

Instruments include a transverse flute, a small hand drum held on the shoulder, a large hand drum held at the hip, and a large drum played with sticks. They enter from *agemaku* (page 93). Some repertoires don't use the large drum.

2

地謡・*jiutai*

Chorus

声をそろえて謡曲をうたう人々のこと。切戸口から出入りする。8人の場合が多い。

A vocal component of Noh music. They usually consist of eight members and enter from the *kiriduguchi*.

3

後見・*koken*
Understudy

曲が始まると、舞台の後ろに控えて能役者を助ける。万が一、役者が舞台を続行できなくなったときに代役を果たす。作り物など道具の出し入れも行う。

Once the music starts, the understudy is seated behind and supports the actor. In case the actor is no longer capable of continuing the performance, the understudy steps in to complete the role. He also helps bringing props on and off stage.

4

作り物・*tsukurimono*
Stage Set

能舞台で用いる大道具。ほとんどは竹組みの簡素なつくりで、家・岩・船・井戸・墓などをシンボリックに表現する。

Commonly made of bamboo. Using the simple structures of a house, rock, boat or gravestone. The props in Noh are highly symbolic.

5

切戸口・*kiridoguchi*
Low Sliding Door

地謡や後見が出入りする、舞台の向かって右奥の小さな出入り口。

Entrance for the chorus members and understudy. Located in the back corner of the right wall of the stage.

能の楽器

笛（能管）、小鼓、大鼓、太鼓の4つの楽器による編成を「四拍子（しびょうし）」という。鼓と太鼓が掛け声をかけながら、役者と対等の立場で能の世界を構築する。

調緒・*shirabeo*
Tuning Cord

桴・*bachi*
Stick

太鼓・*taiko*

Large Drum

鉄の輪に張った2枚の牛皮に胴を挟み、麻の調緒で締めたもの。台に載せて、2本の桴（ばち）で打って演奏する。桴が当たる部分には鹿皮が張ってある。皮を桴で抑えて響かせない打ち方と、大中小と強弱をつけて音を響かせる打ち方がある。

It consists of a body that is taut with two cattle skin drumheads that are stretched over an iron ring and connected by interlaced tuning cords. Placed on a base, it is played with two sticks. The area the sticks hit is covered with deerskin. There are two ways to play this instrument. One is to place the stick on to the head to produce a dull sound and another is to lift the stick to produce a crisp sound, which can vary in the level of loudenss.

Noh Instruments

There are four instruments in the Noh orchestra: a transverse flute, a small hand drum held on the shoulder, a large hand drum held at the hip, and a large drum played with sticks. The cries of the drummers as they hit the drum are also an important musical element. Musicians are as essential as actors in creating the world of Noh.

歌口・*utaguchi*
Embouchure Hole

指孔・*yubiana*
Finger Hole

函・*ie*
Flute Case

笛・*fue*／能管・*nokan*

Flute

煤竹（すすだけ）を8つに割って内外を逆にして筒状にし、漆を塗り重ね、桜の樺を巻いてつくられる。歌口（吹口）と第一指孔の間を切断して、ノド（喉）と呼ばれる竹管を挿入している。これにより、硬質な高音と、吹き込む息の音が多層的に重なって独特の音色をつくる。笛筒（函／いえ）は舞台上でも脇に差している。

After splitting smoked bamboo into 8 pieces and reversing the split strips to place the hard bamboo surface on the inside, they are glued together to form a conical bore. Then, the flute is repeatedly lacquered and bound with thin strips of twisted cherry bark. Between the embouchure hole and the first holes, there is an internal bore restriction made of bamboo inserted. Such structure gives a strong high pitch and unique rich frequency harmonics. Musicians keep their flute case on their belts even on stage.

調緒・*shirabeo*
Tuning Cord

鼓胴・*kodo*
Body

小鼓・*kotsuzumi*

Small Hand Drum

鉄の輪に張った2枚の馬皮に胴を挟み、麻の調緒で締めたもの。左手で調緒を持って右肩に担ぎ、右手で打つ。左手の調緒の扱いと、打つ指の数や位置によって、甲高い音（甲／かん）の強弱、柔らかい音（乙／おつ）の強弱、4種を基本とした音色をつくり出す。

It consists of a body that is taut with two horse skin drumheads that are stretched over an iron ring and connected by interlaced tuning cords. Grasping the cords with the left hand, the musician holds the drum on his right shoulder and hit it with his right hand. By squeezing and releasing the cords, alternating the number of fingers used to tap, and hitting the drum in different areas, one can produce four basic tones: high pitch forte and piano, and soft pitch forte and piano.

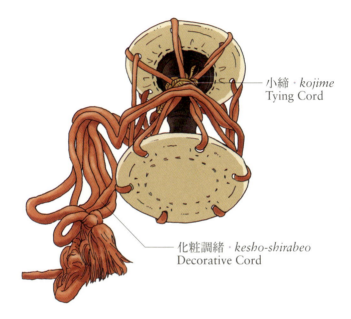

小締・*kojime*
Tying Cord

化粧調緒・*kesho-shirabeo*
Decorative Cord

大鼓・*otsuzumi*

Large Hand Drum

小鼓と同じつくりだが、演奏前に炭火で皮を焙じて硬く乾燥させ、調緒を締め上げ、小締をさらに締めることによって高音を出す。左手で調緒を持って左膝の上に構え、右手で打つ。大鼓は囃子をリードする役割を持つ。

It has the same structure as *kotsuzumi*. By drying the drumheads with charcoal fire beforehand and tying the tuning codes tight, which are then tied with other tying cords, the drum can produce a high pitched tone. Holding the cords with the left hand and placing it on the left knee, musicians play the drum with their right hand. The *otsuzumi* drum leads the orchestra.

雅楽の装束

雅楽とは、日本古来の歌と舞、大陸から伝わった器楽と舞が融合したもの。その伝統的な装束は色鮮やかで、格調高いデザイン性を持つ。ここではその一部を紹介する。

襲装束ー『北庭楽』
Kasane Garments in "Hokuteiraku"

平安時代の武官の正装「束帯（そくたい）」を変化させた装束。袍（ほう）という上着の下に、さまざまな衣装を重ねることから「襲」の名が付いた。

A variation of the formal garments of military officials from the Heian period. *Kasane* means layering in Japanese.

下襲・*shitagasane*
→ p. 103

Gagaku Attire

Gagaku is a type of Japanese classical music in which Japanese ancient singing and dance are fused with instruments and dance from China and Korea. The traditional attire for Gagaku is elegant and colorful. Here are typical examples.

1

袍・*ho*

緋色あるいは緑色の透ける生地に、丸い紋を刺繍した上着。前身頃（まえみごろ）はたくしあげ、後ろ身頃は裾を長く引く。

A round crest is stitched onto scarlet or green semi-translucent fabric. The front is rolled up and the back has a long train.

2

半臂・*hampi*

袍の下に着る、袖なしの胴着。　Sleeveless garment worn underneath *ho*.

3

指貫・*sashinuki*

裾に紐が通してある袴（65頁）のこと。紐で裾をくくり、ふっくらさせる。

A kind of *hakama* (page 65) with strings attached to the hems. Tying the strings creates a billowy form.

4

踏懸・*fugake*

左右の脛（すね）を覆う脚絆（きゃはん）の一種で、指貫の上から着装する。

A kind of gaiter to cover the shins, worn over *sashinuki*.

5

糸鞋・*shikai*

雅楽で用いる履き物。上部を白絹の組糸で編み、底に白革を貼り付けている。

Footwear for Gagaku attire. Woven with twined yarn made of plain non-dyed silk, the sole is made of white leather.

6

鳥甲・*torikabuto*

鳳凰の頭を象った被り物。襲装束を着用する大半の曲で用られる。

Headgear resembling the head of a phoenix. Worn for most of the repertoires played in the *kasane* garments.

蛮絵装束－『長保楽』

Ban-e Garments in "Choboraku"

宮中の警護や行幸の供をする官人が、外出時に着用した装束。袍（ほう／101頁）に蛮絵と呼ばれる向かい獅子の文様が刺繍されている。

Outer wear for court guards and officials attending royal visits. Two lions facing each other are stitched onto the *ho* (page 101).

袍・*ho*
→ p. 101

1
表袴・*uenohakama*

赤大口（あかおおぐち）袴の上につける袴。指貫（101頁）と異なり、裾を括らない。

A *hakama* worn over a red flared *hakama*. Unlike *sashinuki* (page 101), the hems are not tied with strings.

2
下襲・*shitagasane*

袍や半臂（はんぴ／101頁）の下に着る内着。後ろに長い裾が付いている。

Undershirt with a long train, worn under *ho* or *hampi* (page 101).

3
巻纓冠・*ken-ei no kan*

奈良時代や平安時代に朝廷に出仕する官人などが被った冠の一種。冠に付ける飾り（纓／えい）が丸まっているものを巻纓という。

A kind of headgear worn by court officials from the Nara and Heian period. Ones with round-tails are called *ken-ei*.

4
緌（老懸）・*oikake*

武官の冠につけて、顔の左右を覆う扇形の飾り。黒馬の尾毛でつくられている。

Fan shaped ornaments, attached to headgear for military officials. Made of black horsetail, it covers both sides of one's face.

別装束 —『陵王』
Betsu Garments in "Ryo-o"

別装束とは、特定の演目で用いる固有の装束のこと。『陵王』は中国の蘭陵王に由来する。猛々しい仮面で美しさを隠したことにより、兵士の士気が上がって勝利を収めたとされる。

Betsu garments are special garments worn in specific repertoires. "Ryo-o" is a piece based on the story of Prince of Lanling from China. It is said that by hiding his beautiful face with a fierce mask, he was able to uplift his soldiers and win the battle.

袍・*ho*
→ p. 101

指貫・*sashinuki*
→ p. 101

1

裲襠・*ryoto*

布の中央に穴をあけて、頭を通して着る貫頭衣のこと。別装束のなかで、裲襠(りょうとう)を着用するものは「裲襠装束」ともいう。なかでも、この裲襠は唐織で、縁が毛になっているため「毛縁(けべり)裲襠」という。

A single large sheet of fabric with an opening in the center for the head. Among *betsu* garments, the one accompanying *ryoto* is called *ryoto* garments. This particular *ryoto* is woven in a Chinese style with a wool fringe.

2

当帯・*ate-obi*

裲襠の上から締める腰帯。背面に当て、前面に紅色の紐をめぐらして締める。

A belt worn over *ryoto*. Placing the gold plate on the back, the red strings are tied in front.

3

陵王面・*ryo-o-men*

陵王専用の面。上部に龍をいただいたもので、顎や目が動く構造になっている。別装束では面をつける曲が多い。

A mask for "Ryo-o." Featuring a dragon on top, its jaw and eyes are movable. *Betsu* garments often come with specific masks.

4

牟子・*mushi*

頭巾の一種。面をつける際に必ず被って、頭の後ろに垂らす。

A kind of hood worn underneath a mask. It drapes down in the back.

雅楽の装束 ｜ Gagaku Attire

伝統芸能

雅楽の楽器

雅楽には、音楽だけを演奏する曲「管絃」、舞を伴う曲「舞楽（ぶがく）」がある。楽器は西洋音楽と同様に、管楽器（吹物）・絃楽器（弾物）・打楽器（打物）に分類される。

篳篥・*hichiriki*

縦笛の一種。表に7孔、裏に2孔がある竹管。葦（あし）でつくったリードを差し込んで用いる。ほとんどの楽曲に用いられ、主旋律を担当する。高音で、音域は広くない。

A double reed Japanese flute. There are seven finger holes in front and two in the back. It plays the main melodies and is featured in most of the Gagaku repertoire. This instrument produces a small range of high pitched sounds.

笙・*sho*

竹管17本を、檜や桜でつくった椀型の頭（かしら）に差し込んだもの。15本の管につけたさはり製（銅、スズ、鉛の合金）のリードを振動させて和音を奏でる。笙は鳳凰をイメージした形といわれる。

It consists of 17 slender bamboo pipes fitted in its bowl shaped base, made of cypress or cherry wood. Two of the pipes are silent and each of the other 15 pipes has a metal free reed. The shape of the instrument is said to imitate a phoenix.

Gagaku Instruments

Gagaku consists of two primary repertoires: instrumental music and music accompanying dance. Instruments used in Gagaku are classified as wind, string and percussion, similar to western instruments.

高麗笛・*komabue*

横笛の一種。歌口と指孔が6つある。篳篥（ひちりき）より大きく、広い音域を持つ。主に「高麗楽（こまがく）」「右方舞（うほうまい）」という朝鮮系の雅楽に使われる。

A type of transverse flute with six finger holes. It is larger and has a wider range of sound than *hichiriki*. Mainly used in Korean origin repertoire such as *komagaku* and *uhou-mai*.

龍笛・*ryuteki*

横笛の一種。歌口と指孔が7つある。高麗笛より長くて太い。主に「唐楽（とうがく）」「左方舞（さほうまい）」という中国の雅楽で使われる。

A type of transverse flute with seven finger holes. It is longer and thicker than *komabue*. Mainly used in Chinese origin repertoire such as *togaku* and *saho-mai*.

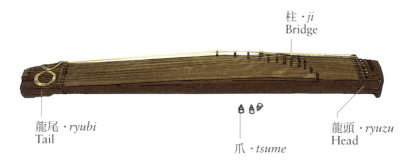

柱・*ji* Bridge
龍尾・*ryubi* Tail
爪・*tsume*
龍頭・*ryuzu* Head

楽箏・*gakuso*

現在の箏のルーツである 13 絃の楽器。構造はほぼ同じで、本体は桐、絃は絹、柱（じ）は紫檀（したん）などでつくられている。音楽だけを演奏する「管絃」にのみ用いられる。

A traditional Japanese stringed musical instrument. Having 13 strings, it is the origin of the *koto*. The body is made of paulownia wood, the strings are silk, and the bridge is made of rosewood. It is only used for instrumental pieces.

爪・*tsume*

指に小さな爪をはめて、楽箏（がくそう）を演奏する。

The strings are plucked using small finger picks.

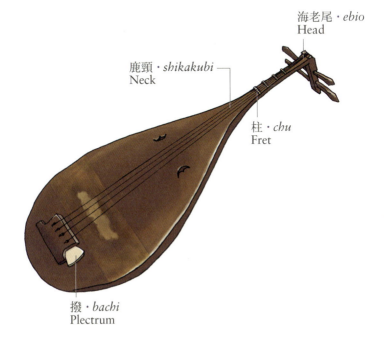

楽琵琶・*gakubiwa*

4絃・4柱の絃楽器。黄楊(つげ)の撥(ばち)を用いて演奏する。奈良時代にペルシアからシルクロードを経て伝来した。楽箏と同様に、管絃にのみ用いられる。

Having four strings and four frets, it is played with a plectrum made of boxwood. The instrument came from Persia via the Silk Road in the Nara period. As with the *gakuso*, it is only used in instrumental repertoire and not used to accompany dancing.

鉦鼓・*shoko*

雅楽で唯一の金属性の楽器。丸い水牛の角が先端についた長い桴(ばち)を、両手で持って打つ。鉦鼓(しょうこ)は片方の桴で1度打つ奏法と、2本で2度打つ奏法がある。打楽器にはほかに「鞨鼓(かっこ)」と「三ノ鼓」があり、形は鼓とほぼ同じだが、桴で打つところが異なる。

The only metal instrument used in Gagaku. Struck with two horn beaters, there are both one-handed and two-handed styles of playing.

釣太鼓・*tsuri-daiko*／楽太鼓・*gaku-daiko*

円形の枠内に吊るされた両面太鼓。皮を巻いた先の丸い桴を両手に持って打つ。管絃にのみ用いられるが、舞楽では舞台上に据えられた2m以上もある「大太鼓（だだいこ）」が用いられる。

A double-faced drum suspended in a round frame. It is struck with two beaters wrapped with leather on top and used only in instrumental music. For dance repertoire, a larger drum called *dadaiko*, which is more than 6 ft. 6 in. tall, is used.

文楽人形と人形遣い

文楽とは、浄瑠璃という語りに合わせて人形を操る芸能で、古くは「人形浄瑠璃」と呼ばれていた。人形遣い、語り手である太夫（たゆう）、三味線奏者が三位一体となって演じる。

1

文楽人形・*bunraku-ningyo*

Bunraku Puppet

首（かしら）、胴部、両手、両足からできている。役柄に合った首を選び、髪を結う。胴部に衣装を縫い付け、手足を取り付け、最後に首をはめる。

Made of a head, torso, and limbs. The main puppeteer selects which head and wig to use for the role. After sewing a costume onto the frame of the puppet and attaching the limbs, the puppeteer inserts the head into the body.

2

主遣い・*omo-zukai*

Main Puppeteer

人形の首と右手を操る人。左手で人形の首を支えながら、頭の動き、顔の表情を操作し、右手で人形の右手を動かす。

Three puppeteers manipulate a single puppet. The main puppeteer operates the head and the right arm. Manipulating the movement of the head and facial expressions of the puppet with his left hand, the puppeteer moves the puppet's right arm with his right hand.

Bunraku Puppet and Puppeteers

Bunraku, which used to be called Ningyo Jyoruri, is a form of traditional Japanese puppet theater combining spoken and sung narration called Jyoruri. The performance involves puppeteers, a narrator called *tayu*, and *shamisen* players.

3

舞台下駄 · *butai-geta*

Stage Clogs

主遣いが舞台下駄を履くことで、足遣いが楽に動けるようにする。

Worn by the main puppeteer, it allows the third puppeteer to move easily.

4

左遣い · *hidari-zukai*

Second Puppeteer

人形の左手を操る人。左手で人形の腰を支え、右手で人形の左手を操作する。同時に、人形が使う小道具の出し入れも行う。

Holding the puppet waist with the left hand, the second puppeteer operates its left arm with the right hand. The puppeteer is also in charge of handling the props for the puppet.

5

足遣い · *ashi-zukai*

Third Puppeteer

人形の足を操る人。女の人形は足がないため、着物の裾さばきで表現する。動きによって、自分の足を踏みならして足拍子をとる。

The third puppeteer operates the puppet feet. Female puppets have no legs and the movement of their feet and legs are simulated by moving the hem of their kimono. Sometime the puppeteer uses his own feet to render certain movements of the puppet.

黒衣 · *kurogo*

Black Suit

足遣いと左遣いは黒い衣装で黒頭巾を被る。黒衣は存在しないことを暗示する。歌舞伎でも役者の手助けをしたり、小道具を用意したりする。

The second and third puppeteers are dressed in black and their heads are covered by hoods to remain inconspicuous. In Kabuki, stagehands are called *kurogo*.

文楽の舞台

人形遣いが人形を操る舞台の向かって右に、浄瑠璃を語る太夫と三味線奏者が座る床（ゆか）がある。

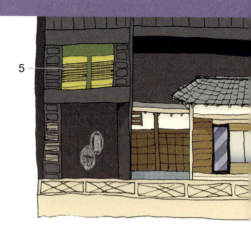

___1
太夫・*tayu*
Narrator

浄瑠璃を語る人。浄瑠璃とは、日本の音楽の一種で、物語に節をつけて語る芸能。江戸時代に浄瑠璃語りに秀でた竹本義太夫（ぎだゆう）が登場してから、浄瑠璃は義太夫とも呼ばれる。

The narration for Bunraku is called Jyoruri and involves a narrator singing with musical accompaniment. After the appearance of Takemoto Gidayu who was a great Jyoruri narrator from the Edo period, Jyoruri also became known as Gidayu.

___2
三味線（文楽）・*shamisen*
Shamisen Players

太棹の三味線（146頁）を構えて、太夫の語りに合わせて弾く人。

Shamisen with a thick neck (page 146) are used to accompany the narration.

___3
見台・*kendai*
Bookstand

書物をのせて読む台のこと。文楽では床本（ゆかほん）と呼ばれる手書きの台本をのせる。太夫は床本に書かれたすべての登場人物のセリフと地の文を一人で語る。

Place to rest the handwritten script. One narrator sings and speaks the voices for all the dialogue and narration.

Bunraku Stage

The narrator and *shamisen* players are located on a revolving stage to the right.

4
床・*yuka*
Revolving Stage

回転式の床。開幕すると、無人の床が半周して、太夫と三味線が登場する。場面が変わるごとに、次に登場する太夫と三味線が、後ろに控えていて入れ替わる。

Once the curtain is raised, the stage revolves and the narrator and *shamisen* players make their appearances. The narrator and the musicians for the next scene stand by on the other half of the stage in the back before the stage revolves again.

5
御簾・*misu*
Bamboo Blind

室内の開口部や窓に掛ける、竹ひごなどを編んでつくられた簾(すだれ)のこと。文楽の舞台では、向かって右手の御簾の内側に若手の太夫と三味線が控え、つなぎの場面などの浄瑠璃(義太夫)を務める。左手の御簾の内側では、太鼓や鐘などの鳴物が演奏される。

Behind the blind to the right sit a junior narrator and *shamisen* players who take part in the beginning scenes. Behind the blind to the left are the percussionists.

歌舞伎の装束

歌舞伎とは江戸時代の町人文化として花開いた伝統芸能。男役、女役関係なく、歌舞伎役者はすべて男性。様式美にあふれた衣装から、江戸時代の身分に応じた装束まで紹介する。

つっころばし－『恋飛脚大和往来』忠兵衛
Tsukkorobashi – Chube in "Koibikyaku Yamato Orai"

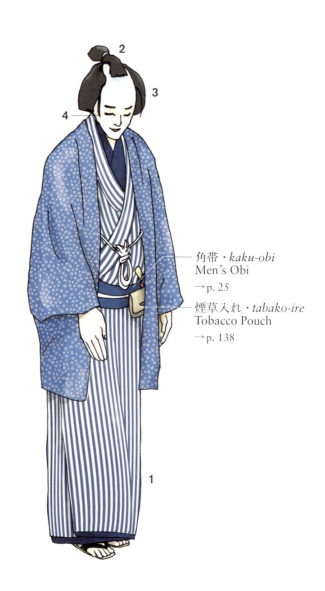

角帯・*kaku-obi*
Men's Obi
→ p. 25

煙草入れ・*tabako-ire*
Tobacco Pouch
→ p. 138

Kabuki Costumes

Kabuki is a traditional Japanese performing art, fostered in the flourishing culture of the townspeople and merchant class of the Edo period. All roles are played by men. Here are examples of the stylized costumes as well as the costumes of everyday people of the time.

「つっころばし」とは、庶民の生活を描いた世話物によく登場する、世間知らずな気の優しい若旦那のこと。肩を突っ込むと倒れてしまいそうなことを言い表している。

A *tsukkorobashi* is an heir to fortune who is kind but ignorant of the real world. This type of character often appears in plays that depict everyday life in the Edo period. The name means someone who would easily fall when poked on the shoulder.

1

着流し・*kinagashi*
Kimono without *Hakama*

男性の日常の装い方で、袴をつけない。イラストは縞の着物に、小紋（21頁）の羽織（65頁）を纏っている。

Everyday wear for men. Here is a stripe kimono and a *haori* (page 65) in the *komon* style (page 21).

2

丁髷・*chon-mage*
Men's Topknot

男性の日本髪の一種。頭頂部の髪を剃りあげ、余った髪を束ねて折り曲げた髪型のこと。頭髪を剃りあげた部分を月代（さかやき）といい、束ねた髪の部分のことを髷という。

A form of Japanese traditional haircut worn by men. Featuring a shaved pate, the remaining hair is oiled and tied into a small ponytail, called *mage*, which is folded onto the top of the head.

3

鬢・*bin*
Sidelocks

顔の両サイドの髪。

A lock of hair falling at the side of the face.

4

しけ・*shike*
Loose Hair

髪が乱れて、鬢から垂れた一筋の髪のこと。

A strand of hair coming out from one's sidelocks.

歌舞伎の装束 | Kabuki Costumes

伝統芸能

武士―『寿曾我対面』曾我五郎時致

Samurai – Soga Goro Tokimune in "Kotobuki Soga no Taimen"

時代物（歴史的事件を主題とした演目）の主役となる武士の装束は、その時代と役柄によって多種多様。イラストのような裃（かみしも）と袴姿は、時代物では一般的な装束である。

Costumes for the main samurai characters for historical repertoire vary in time and according to each character. Here is a typical example.

1

裃（上下）・*kamishimo*

Formal Wear for Samurai

武士の礼装で、肩衣（かたぎぬ）という上衣と袴（65頁）という下衣のセットのこと。室町時代からある装束で、江戸時代の肩衣は肩幅が広くなり、衿を重ねないような形に変化した。

It is a traditional suit consisting of an upper garment called, *kataginu*, and a *hakama* (page 65).

2

長袴・*naga-bakama* ／ 引袴・*hiki-bakama*

Long Divided Skirt

裾が足よりも長く、引きずるようにして履く袴のこと。イラストのような長袴と肩衣の裃を「長裃」という。足首までの半袴の場合は「半裃」という。

A *hakama* with a long train. One trails it on the floor when walking. The illustration shows a *naga-kamishimo*.

3

隈取・*kumadori* ／ むきみ隈・*mukimi-kuma*

Kumadori Makeup

隈取とは歌舞伎特有の化粧のこと。荒事（あらごと）と呼ばれる豪快な様式美が特徴の演目でよく見られる、血管や筋肉の隆起を誇張して描かれたもの。さまざまな隈取があり、青い隈取は悪役を表すなど、ひと目でその人物の素性がわかる。イラストの「むきみ隈」は正義感のある若々しい男前の役に用いられる。

The distinctive Kabuki style of makeup, often worn for the bold and bombastic *aragoto* repertoires. It exaggerates veins and musculature. Specific makeup depends on the characters – a blue *kumadori* is for ruthless villains, and the audience can have some understanding of the character at a glance. Here is the makeup for a righteous young handsome man.

腹出し－『暫』成田五郎

Haradashi – Narita Goro in "Shibaraku"

「腹出し」とは敵（かたき）役のこと。赤い腹を出していることから名が付いた。冷酷な大悪人を「実悪（じつあく）」というのに対し、その家来である腹出しのような悪役は「端敵（はがたき）」という。

Haradashi is a minor villain in Kabuki. The name comes from the fact they are exposing their red bellies. Ruthless villains are called *jitsuaku*, while their servants like *haradashi* are called *hagataki*.

1

赤っ面・*akattsura*

Red Face

顔を赤く塗る化粧のこと。もしくはそのような化粧をする人物。腹出しのような端敵によく使われる。

Refers to makeup that covers actors' faces in red or a character who wears such makeup. Usually worn by minor villains like *hagataki*.

2

着肉・*chakuniku*

Body Suit

衣裳の下に着用するものの総称。刺青の柄が入った「刺青着肉」や、白粉を塗ったように白い「おしろい着肉」など、さまざまな種類がある。

Worn underneath Kabuki costumes, it represents the character's skin. There are various types such as those with tattoos or in white, which makes it look as if the actor has powdered skin when worn.

3

肉襦袢・*niku-juban*

Muscle Body Suit

綿を入れて太らせた着肉の通称。体格の大きな役を演じる際によく用いられる。

A type of *chakuniku*, padded with cotton. It is worn for a large well-built character.

4

三里当て・*sanriate*

Triangular Cloth

「三里」というツボに灸（きゅう）を据えた跡を隠すために膝下に巻いた三角布のこと。江戸時代の庶民の移動手段は徒歩が基本であったため、足の疲労回復に効くという膝の外側のツボ「三里」に灸を据えたという。

Tied just below the knees to cover the marks from burning mugwort on acupressure points. Since walking was the means of mobility for the people of the Edo period, they used to burn mugwort on acupressure points to relieve aches and pains in the legs.

5

板鬢・*ita-bin*

Flared Sidelocks

左右に張り出させて固めた板のような鬢（びん）のこと。鬢付け油で磨き上げてつくる。荒事（あらごと）でよく使われる髪形で、力強さを表す。

Hardened with Japanese pomade, this dynamic hairstyle is often featured in *aragoto* repertoire.

歌舞伎の装束 ━ Kabuki Costumes

伝統芸能

赤姫－『妹背山婦女庭訓』橋姫

Akahime – Hashihime in "Imoseyama Onna Teikin"

歌舞伎の姫役は赤い着物を着ていることが多いことから「赤姫」と呼ばれる。純情でありながら情熱的な若い女性にふさわしい格好である。

Aka means red in Japanese and since princesses often wear red kimono in Kabuki, *akahime* became a general term for princess. Red represents innocent yet passionate and romantic characteristics of young women.

懐紙・*kaishi*
Paper Napkin
→ p. 43

振袖・*furisode*
Formal Kimono
for Unmarried Women
→ p. 17

1

しごき帯・*shigoki-obi*／抱え帯・*kakae-obi*
Waistband

長い裾をたくし上げて、引きずらないようにするための布。江戸時代の高貴な女性は、基本的に着物の裾を引いて屋内を歩くが、外出時は汚れないようにしごき帯を使って裾の長さを調節していた。

A strip of cloth to tuck up the long train of a kimono. Noble women from the Edo period usually trailed their kimono indoors. When going out, they used a waistband to adjust the length of their kimono.

2

丸ぐけ・*maruguke*
Maruguke Obi Belt

帯締め（28頁）の一種で、布で綿を包んでつくる細長い紐。歌舞伎では丸ぐけしか用いない。

A type of *obi-jime* (page 28) made of cotton wrapped in fabric. This is the only type of obi belt used in Kabuki performances.

3

吹き輪銀の前ざし・*fukiwa gin no maezashi*
Silver Hairpin for Princess

赤姫定番の髪型「吹き輪」の前方につけた大きな簪（かんざし）のこと。イラストの銀の前ざしは花をかたどっている。銀といっても、歌舞伎で使われる髪飾りはほとんどが紙と布でできている。

A large Japanese hair ornament placed in a princess's hair. Here is a flower motif. Though it has "silver" in its name, for the stage, most of them are made of paper and fabric.

歌舞伎の装束　Kabuki Costumes

伝統芸能

町娘―『松竹梅雪曙』八百屋お七

Machi-musume – Yaoya Oshichi in "Shochikubai Yuki no Akebono"

町娘とは、町人の娘など庶民の女子のこと。赤姫（122頁）が豪奢な柄入りの着物であるのに対して、町娘は縞（54頁）や格子（56頁）、小紋（21頁）の着物が多い。

A *machi-musume* is an ordinary girl. Compared to an *akahime*'s decorative kimono (page 122), *machi-musume* usually wear kimono with stripes (page 54), grids (page 56) and *komon* (page 21).

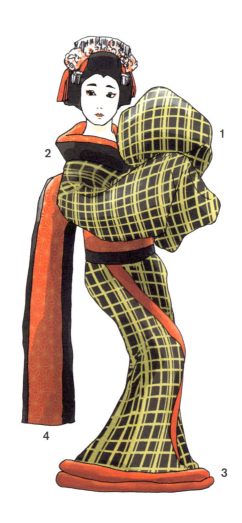

1

黄八丈・*kihachijo*
Striped or Checkered Yellow Kimono

黄色地に鳶（とび）色や弁柄色（45頁）の縞や格子が入った絹織物。元々、八丈島で染めて織られていたことからのネーミング。

A silk kimono with stripe and grid patterns of dark brown with a tint of red, and *bengara-iro* (page 45). The name comes from the fact that the fabric was originally produced on Hachijo Island.

2

黒衿・*kuro-eri*
Black Collar

黒い掛衿（14頁）のこと。着物の衿が鬢付け油で汚れないように黒衿をつけたことが始まりで、江戸時代にはオシャレの1つにもなった。

Originally a cover to protect collars (page 14) from hair oil stains. Later, they became a fashionable trend in the Edo period.

3

ふき綿・*fukiwata*
Overlay Hem

真綿が入った着物の裾のこと。着物の裏地を表に折り返して、綿を入れて厚みを出している。表地の裾の傷みや汚れを防ぐために始まったとされ、おもりの役割も果たしている。

The liner of the kimono turned up to the front and stuffed with floss silk creates a solid hemline. It is said to have been developed to protect the hem from damage and staining. It also gives a nice weight to the bottom of the kimono.

4

振り下げ・*furisage*
Hanging Obi Knot

帯結び（26頁）の一種で、帯の両端を長く垂らした結び方。歌舞伎では帯の結び目を形よく見せるために、胴に回している部分と垂らしている部分に、別々の帯を用いている。

A variation of the obi knot (page 26) in which the long ends of an obi drape down loosely. In order to emphasize the knot, two separate obi are used for the belt and the drape in Kabuki.

歌舞伎の装束 ｜ Kabuki Costumes

伝統芸能

花魁－『籠釣瓶花街酔醒』八ツ橋

Oiran – Yatsuhashi in "Kagotsurube Sato no Eizame"

花魁（おいらん）とは、教養と美貌を兼ね備えたトップクラスの遊女のこと。豪華絢爛な着物や髪飾りをしていた遊女たちは、江戸時代のファッションリーダー的存在だった。

Oiran is an exalted rank of courtesan, educated and beautiful. Dressed in glamorous kimono and hairstyles, they often set trends in the Edo period.

1

まないた帯・*manaita-obi*

Oiran Obi

花魁が「花魁道中」で締める帯のこと。細かい刺繍や織りの華やかさを主張するように、前に結ぶ。江戸時代の大名の妻や裕福な女性も前結びをしていたが、帯の幅が広がるにつれ、結び目が動作の邪魔になるために後ろで結ぶようになった。

Worn when an *oiran* parades between her lodging house and a teahouse to escort her guests. In order to show off the detail and beauty of the weaving and embroidery, it is tied in front.

2

道中着・*dochugi*

Oiran Procession Kimono

「花魁道中」の際に着る華やかな着物。花魁道中とは、新造などの見習い遊女らを引き連れて、ひいきの客を迎えに行くこと。座敷では道中着に比べて落ち着いた着物を着ている。

A highly decorative kimono worn when an *oiran* parades between her lodging house and a teahouse. She is accompanied by child apprentices and younger courtesans in a grand procession. *Oiran* wears more subtle kimono in the banquet room.

3

鼈甲の髪飾り・*bekko no kamikazari*

Tortoiseshell Hair Ornaments

花魁をはじめとして、遊女は鼈甲（べっこう）の簪（かんざし）や笄をたくさん使った豪奢な髪型にしていた。鼈甲は熱帯に棲むウミガメの一種・タイマイの甲羅の加工品。高級品のため、馬の爪でつくられた馬爪（ばず）櫛と呼ばれる模倣品が出回ったという。

Prostitutes, including *oiran*, wear decorative hairstyles using many ornaments made of tortoiseshell. Tortoiseshell is a material produced from the hawksbill sea turtle in tropical regions. Since it is a luxury product, replicas made of horse nails were popular stand-ins.

4

三歯下駄・*samba-geta*

Wooden Clogs with Three Platforms

三本の歯がついた、20cm以上高さのある下駄。花魁道中で履く下駄で、非常に重い。花魁は足を滑らせるように、八文字を描いてゆっくりと歩く。

Worn when an *oiran* parades to escort her guests, it is more than 8 in. tall and very heavy to walk with. *Oiran* walk slowly in a very distinctive gait.

歌舞伎の装束 — Kabuki Costumes

伝統芸能

歌舞伎の髪飾り

江戸時代の女性は髷（まげ）を結う際に、さまざまな髪飾りを用いる。歌舞伎では被り物を見れば、その人の素性がわかる。ここでは、髪飾りと被り物の一部を紹介する。

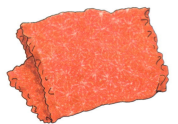

鹿の子絞りの布
Kanoko Tie-dye Fabric

結綿・*yuiwata*

日本髪の一種で、若い未婚の娘がよく結う髪型。島田髷という髪型をベースに、鹿の子（かのこ）絞りなどの布切れが掛けられている。ほかにも既婚女性が結う髷があり、髪型を見ればどのような立場の女性かがわかった。

A form of Japanese hairstyle for young unmarried women. *Kanoko* tie-dye fabric covers a topknot of the *shimada* style. Married women wear their hair differently and the audience can identify them clearly.

Kabuki Hair Ornaments

Women from the Edo period used various ornaments in their hair. In Kabuki, the audience can learn about the character by looking at their headgear. Here are typical examples.

1
元結・*mottoi (motoyui)*

髪をまとめるための紐や糸のこと。近世は紙を縒ったものが主流となった。

Strings and threads to tie one's hair with. They were commonly made of paper in the Edo period.

2
丈長・*takenaga*

和紙製の髪飾りの一種。

A type of hair ornaments made of *washi* paper.

3
つまみ簪・*tsumami-kanzashi*

球状のつまみ細工がついた簪（かんざし）。つまみ細工とは、薄い布や紙を小さくつまんで糊付けしていき、動植物などをかたどった伝統的な手芸のこと。

A hairpin with a kind of ball made in a traditional craft called *tsumami-zaiku*. Thin fabric and paper are pinched tightly and glued to create floral and animal motifs.

角隠し・*tsunokakushi*
揚帽子・*age-boshi*

Headwear

塵除けのために被る、外出用の帽子。布の中央を前髪に被せ、両端を髷の後ろに回してとめる。明治以降は婚礼の際に花嫁が被るものになった（62頁）。

Worn to protect one's hair from dust when on an outing. The center of the cloth covers one's forehead and both ends are tied in the back. It evolved into headwear for a bride at a wedding ceremony (page 62) after the Meiji period.

紫帽子・
murasaki-boshi

Purple Headwear

歌舞伎で用いられる、額の生え際に当てる紫縮緬（ちりめん）の小さな布のこと。江戸時代の歌舞伎の女方が、鬘と生え際をきれいに始末できないために隠したことから始まったとされる。

A small piece of crepe fabric placed on the hairline. It is said to have been used to hide the unkempt hairline of the male actors who played women's roles in the Edo period.

紫鉢巻・
murasaki-hachimaki
Purple Headband

紫縮緬の鉢巻のことで、右に結んでいる場合、力強い伊達男の印になる。歌舞伎十八番『助六由縁江戸桜』の主人公・助六が紫鉢巻をしている。歌舞伎十八番とは、市川團十郎家にゆかりの深い演目のこと。

Made of crepe fabric. When tied on the right side of the actor's head, it indicates a vibrant and elegant man. Worn by Sukeroku from "Sukeroku Yukari no Edo Zakura."

病鉢巻・
yamai-hachimaki
Ailing Headband

紫鉢巻を左に結んでいる場合、病鉢巻という。病気患いや恋患いを表している。

When the purple headband is tied on the left side of the actor's head, it indicates an ailing person. The cause of the illness can be an actual diseases or simply lovesickness.

歌舞伎の舞台

様式美にあふれた派手な演出が多い歌舞伎。舞台には、さまざまな仕掛けや演出がある。

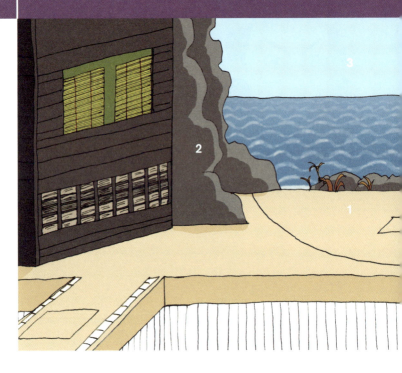

1
廻り舞台・*mawari-butai*
Revolving Stage

舞台上に仕組まれた円形舞台を180度回転させることによって、場面転換をする仕掛け。江戸時代中期の1758年、世界に先がけて発明使用された。

Part of the stage is cut out in a circle, which turns to change scenes quickly. It was invented in 1758 and was the first of its kind in the world.

2
書割・*kakiwari*
Background Scenery

木や岩など、背景として描かれ、舞台に立てられた大道具。

It is part of the stage set and depicts the background view such as trees and rocks.

Kabuki Stage

There are many devices and effects on a Kabuki stage, all intended to help create a highly stylized performance.

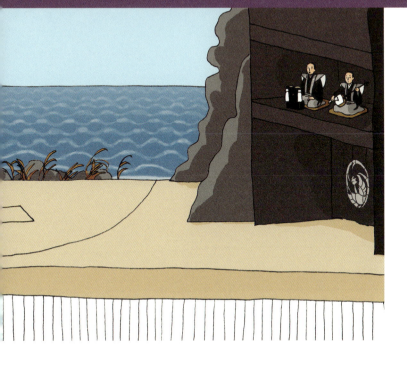

3

遠見・*tomi*
Distant Scenery

遠景の書割のことを、特に遠見という。

A type of *kakiwari* that depicts a distant view.

引幕・*hikimaku*／定式幕・*joshikimaku*
Main Curtain

芝居の始まりと終わりに引く幕のこと。特に歌舞伎や文楽で用いられる黒・柿色・緑の3色縦縞の幕を定式幕という。

Pulled open and closed to mark the beginning and the end of performances. The distinctive one with three stripes of black, dark orange and green, called *joshikimaku*, is used for Kabuki and Bunraku.

133

上手
Stage Left

上手・*kamite*

Stage Left

客席から見て舞台の中央より右側のこと。上座（かみざ）にあたるため、通常、身分の高い人が座る。

From the audience's perspective, the right half of the stage. It is considered to be a seat of honor and usually people of high status take their position here.

1

竹本・*takemoto*

Narrator and *Shamisen* Player

義太夫（浄瑠璃）を語る太夫と三味線を演奏する人のこと。浄瑠璃の名手、竹本義太夫の名前から竹本と呼んで、文楽と区別している。

In Kabuki, the combination of a narrator and *shamisen* player who perform Jyoruri (or Gidayu) is called *takemoto*, in order to distinguish it from Bunraku.

2

ちょぼ床・*choboyuka*

Takemoto Seat

舞台の上手上部に設けられた、竹本が座る床のこと。御簾（みす）が下がった状態で演奏することが多いが、イラストのように竹本が姿を見せて演奏することを「出語り」という。

Located on the upper side of stage left. *Takemoto* mostly perform behind a bamboo blind but sometimes appear on stage as shown here.

3

揚幕（歌舞伎）・*agemaku*

Actor's Curtain

役者の出入り口に掛かっている幕。花道（137頁）の出入り口にもある。

Actors come on and off stage from this curtain. There is also one at the end of the *hanamichi* (page 137) as well.

下手
Stage Right

下手・*shimote*

Stage Right

客席から見て舞台の中央より左側のこと。左端が役者の出入り口となる。

From the audience's perspective, the left half of the stage. Actors enter the stage from stage right.

1

黒御簾・*kuro-misu*
Black Blind

舞台下手の黒い御簾（みす）が掛けられた一角のこと。この内側で下座（げざ）音楽（146頁）を演奏している。

Located at stage right, many instruments in addition to the *shamisen* (page 146) are played behind the blind.

2

花道・*hanamichi*
Runway

舞台から客席後方に向かってのびる長い廊下のこと。歌舞伎にとって重要な演劇空間で、役者の見せ場でもある。上手にも花道を設置して「両花道」にする演出もある。

A long passage running through the left side of auditorium. It is a very important theatrical element in Kabuki. A variation with *hanamichi* on both sides can be seen.

3

迫り・*seri*
Stage Lift

役者を舞台下から舞台上に出現させる仕掛け。奈落（ならく）と呼ばれる舞台の下から昇降機に乗って迫り上がってくる。

A device used to raise actors up to the stage from the *naraku*, the space below. This elevating device creates a dynamic atmosphere.

4

すっぽん・*suppon*
Runway Stage Lift

花道の舞台寄り、七三（しちさん）と呼ばれる場所にある迫りのこと。妖怪や幽霊など人間離れした存在がここから登場する。

A form of *seri*, located in the runway close to the stage. It is used for the appearance of ghosts and other supernatural beings.

歌舞伎の小道具

歌舞伎には江戸時代の風習がわかる小道具が多く登場する。ここでは、その一部を紹介する。

根付・*netsuke*
Fastener
→p. 140

煙管・*kiseru*
Tobacco Pipe

先端の火皿に刻み煙草を詰めて、吸う道具。歌舞伎では役柄によって煙管の持ち方が異なる。

A traditional Japanese pipe used for smoking a finely shredded tobacco product stuffed in the bowl. The way of holding the pipe varies depending on the character.

煙草入れ・*tabako-ire*
Tobacco Pouch

刻み煙草や煙管を入れておく袋。イラストは「提げ煙草入れ」といって、腰に提げて持ち歩くもの。

It holds shredded tobacco and a pipe. Here is a type that is worn around the waist.

煙管筒・*kiseru-zutsu*
Pipe Case

煙管を入れておく筒のこと。煙管筒と煙草入れを根付(140頁)につける「両提げ」、煙管筒を帯に直接差し込む「筒差し」など、持ち運び方はさまざまである。

To transport one's pipe, some hang it with *netsuke* (page 140) and others insert it directly into their obi sash.

Kabuki Props

Many Kabuki props have much to tell us about customs from the Edo period. Here are some examples.

煙管・*kiseru*
Tabacco Pipe

1

煙草盆・*tabako-bon*
Tobacco Tray

火入や灰吹、煙管などを入れておく盆。

A box to store a kindling container, an ashtray and a pipe.

2

灰吹・*haifuki*
Ashtray

煙草の灰や吸殻を落とし込む筒のこと。多くは竹製。

Usually made of bamboo, it has a cylindrical shape.

3

火入・*hi-ire*
Kindling Container

火種の炭と灰を入れておく器。

A container to hold coals and ash for lighting a pipe.

139

緒締・*ojime*

印籠・*inro*

Lacquered Pill Case

江戸時代の武士が腰に提げていた漆塗りの薬入れ。もしくは実用を伴わないアクセサリーで、男性のオシャレの1つ。室町時代では印鑑を持ち歩くためのものだった。

Samurai from the Edo period carried these as pill cases but also as fashionable accessories. In the Muromachi period, people used to carry their personal seal in them.

根付・*netsuke*

Fastener

印籠（いんろう）や煙草入れなどの紐の先端につける装飾品。根付を帯に挟んで、腰から印籠や煙草入れなどを提げる。多種多様なデザインがあり、世界的なコレクションアイテムの1つになっている。

A carved, button-like fastener used to secure the cords of containers such as pill cases and tobacco pouches. Passing through the obi sash, it fastens hanging containers to the waist. With a wide variety of designs, they have become a very collectable item internationally.

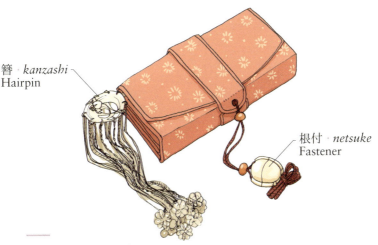

簪・*kanzashi*
Hairpin

根付・*netsuke*
Fastener

筥迫・*hakoseko*

Purse

女性が懐紙（43頁）、鏡、髪飾り、櫛などを入れて懐中するための小物入れ。

It holds paper napkins (page 43), mirrors, hair ornaments and combs, and women carry it in the bosom of their kimono.

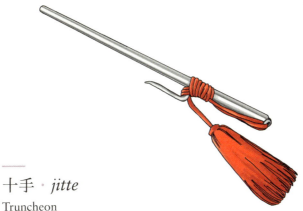

十手・*jitte*

Truncheon

捕吏が罪人を捕らえるために用いた武器。相手を攻撃したり、相手の刀を防いだりする。柄と鉤（かぎ）に房付きの紐がついているが、その色によって身分や所属がわかった。

A weapon used by police in the Edo period to capture criminals. Not only it can deliver an attack, but it was also used to block the opponent's sword. The color of tasseled cord on the handle and the hook varies depending on the owners' status.

番傘 · *bangasa*

Heavy Japanese Umbrella

江戸時代の庶民が使った和傘。丈夫な竹の骨に和紙を張って油を引き、やや太い竹の柄をつけていた。

Used by ordinary people from the Edo period. Oiled *washi* paper is affixed over a stout bamboo frame. The handle is thicker than on a *janomegasa*.

蛇の目傘 · *janomegasa*

Japanese Umbrella

傘を開いたときに同心円が見える傘。その模様を蛇の目に見立てたところからのネーミング。近代には、蛇の目がなくても、柄の細い和傘をこう呼ぶようになった。

Janome means a snake's eye in Japanese and it refers to the concentric circle inside the umbrella. Today, any umbrella with a skinny handle is called *janomegasa* even without the concentric circle.

合掌鏡台
gassho-kyodai
Mirror Stand

合わせ鏡ができるように、2枚の鏡がのった台。合わせ鏡を使って衿足などを見られるようになっており、歌舞伎では化粧をしているシーンなどで登場する。

It comes with two mirrors, which allows a lady to check her neckline. Used in makeup scenes.

角火鉢
kaku-hibachi
Brazier

庶民の家によく見られる、四角い木枠の火鉢。金属製のもの、湯呑を置くスペースや引き出しのある「長火鉢」、またがって暖をとるための「股火鉢」などさまざまな種類がある。

A square wooden brazier is often seen in ordinary people's houses in Kabuki.

すし桶 · *sushi-oke*
Sushi Bucket

「熟(な)れ寿司」を入れた木製の桶のこと。この桶に塩漬けの魚とご飯を交互に入れて発酵させてつくる。歌舞伎では、鮎の熟れ寿司を商う、奈良県・吉野のつるべ鮨屋が有名。

A wooden container for fermented sushi in which salted fish and rice are layered alternately. Tsurube Sushi in Yoshino, Nara who sells fermented sushi with *Ayu* fish is a signature shop in Kabuki.

酒樽 · *saka-daru*
Sake Barrel

酒の入った木製の樽のこと。江戸時代は仕込んだ酒を樽に入れて、客が必要な分だけ徳利などに量り売りしていた。

In the Edo period, sake was stored in wooden barrels and sold in bulk. People brought their own containers such as *tokkuri* to the stores to purchase sake.

歌舞伎の楽器

三味線をメインに、演目によって太鼓、鼓、笛（96-99頁）などが演奏される。黒御簾（137頁）の中では、BGMとなる「下座（げざ）音楽」と、さまざまな効果音をつくる「鳴物道具」が奏でられる。

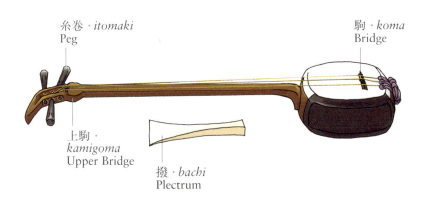

三味線・*shamisen*

弦楽器の一種。猫や犬の皮を張った胴に棹をつけて、3本の弦を張ったもの。撥（ばち）で弦をはじいて演奏する。16世紀後半に、中国の楽器「三弦（さんげん）」が琉球（沖縄）を経由して堺（大阪）に渡ったとされる。日本に伝来後、改良を重ねて今の形になった。

A traditional Japanese stringed instrument. It consists of a neck and body with cat and dog skin with three strings stretched across it. The *shamisen* is played with a plectrum called *bachi*. It is believed that the Chinese instrument sanxian was introduced though the Ryukyu, today's Okinawa, in the late 16th century and this ancestor of *shamisen* traveled to Sakai, Osaka. The instrument evolved from there.

Kabuki Instruments

Featuring *shamisen* as a main instrument, drums, hand drums and flutes (page 96-99) are also played depending on the repertoire. Background music called *geza* music and various sound effects are played behind the blind (page 137) to the left.

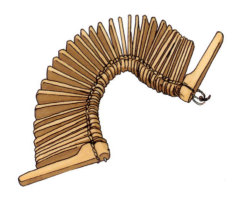

びんざさら・*binzasara*

紐で連ねた数十枚の木片の両側に柄をつけて、両手で開閉して音を出す。田植えのときの舞踊から発達した田楽（でんがく）に用いられた道具。

Many pieces of wooden plates strung together with a string. The sound is produced by opening and closing the handles at both ends. This percussion instrument was used for Dengaku, a dance to celebrate rice planting.

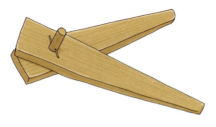

艪の音・*ro no oto*

手漕ぎ船が水面を進むときの艪（ろ）の音を出す道具。

An instrument to produce the sound of a Japanese boat oar when proceeding through the water.

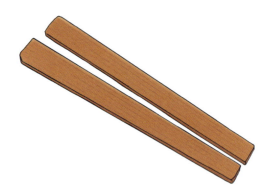

笏拍子・*shaku-byoshi*

笏（69頁）を縦2つに割った楽器。T字型に打ち合わせて音を出す。本来は雅楽の楽器だが、歌舞伎では王朝をテーマとした演目などに用いる。

A percussion instrument made of a *shaku*, wooden mace (page 69), that is split in half. The percussionists hit the two bars in a T shape. It is a Gagaku instrument but also used for Kabuki's repertoire based on the imperial era.

撞木・*shumoku*
Beater

盤木・*bangi*

本来、寺院などで合図や時報として打つもの。火災や騒動などを知らせるときにも打つ。歌舞伎を盛り立てる場で使う。

Primarily used as a cue to mark events and tell time at temples, as well as to inform of fires and civil uproar, it is played to bring excitement to scenes in Kabuki.

雨団扇 · *ame-uchiwa*

ビーズが糸でつけられた団扇。雨団扇を振って、打ちつける雨の音を表現する。

Beads on the strings are attached to a Japanese fan. Waving the fan produces the sound of heavy rain.

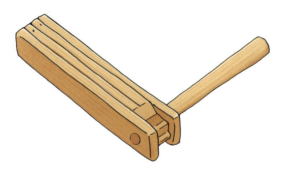

がり時計 · *garidokei*

昔の時計の音を出す道具。木車を回して、ゼンマイの音を表現する。

An instrument to produce the sound of an old clock. Turning the wheel makes the sound of winding up a mainspring.

INDEX

和服
JAPANESE TRADITIONAL CLOTHING

あ	藍色	*ai-iro*	48
	揚羽蝶	Swallowtail Butterfly	59
	浅葱色	*asagi-iro*	47
	麻の葉	Flax Leaf	51
	網代	Wicker	50
	洗朱	*araishu*	44
	市松模様	Checkered Pattern	56
	色無地	Single-colored Kimono	20
	鶯色	*uguisu-iro*	46
	打掛	Robe	63
	馬乗袴	Divided Skirt	65
	鱗	Scale	50
	上指糸	Decorative Thread	69
	江戸紫	*edo-murasaki*	49
	烏帽子	Headgear	68
	衿	Collar	12
	衿先	*eri-saki*	14
	臙脂色	*enji-iro*	45
	黄丹	*oni*	45
	翁格子	*Okina* Plaid	57
	衽	*okumi*	15
	おはしょり	Tuck	13
	帯揚げ	Obi Bustle	28
	帯板	*obi-ita*	32
	帯締め	Obi Belt	28
	帯留め	Obi Clip	29
	帯枕	*obi-makura*	32
か	貝の口	*kai no kuchi*	27
	角帯	Men's Obi	25
	掛衿	*kake-eri*	14

掛下	Under Robe Kimono	63
籠目	Reticulum	51
重ね衿	Layered Collar	13
菓子楊枝と懐紙	Pick and Paper Napkin	43
絣	Ikat Kimono	22
合切袋	Large Drawstring Bag	36
唐紅色（韓紅色）	*kara-kurenai-iro*	44
狩衣	*Kariginu* Ceremonial Kimono	68
桔梗	Balloon Flower	58
亀甲	Hexagon	51
切袴	Divided Skirt for Shinto Priest	69
巾着	Drawstring Bag	36
紅色（くれないいろ）	*kurenai-iro*	44
軍配団扇	Referee's Fan	71
袈裟	Monk's Stole	67
化粧回し	Ceremonial Loincloth	70
香色	*ko-iro*	46
五三ノ桐	Five and Three Paulownia	58
駒下駄	Wooden Clogs	34
小紋	Finely Patterned Kimono	21
差袴	Divided Skirt for Shinto Priest	69
作務衣	Monk's Work Clothes	67
侍烏帽子	Samurai Headgear	71
紗綾形	Modified Fylfot	52
地下足袋	Rubber-soled Socks	73
直綴	Monk's Robe	67
七宝繋ぎ	Gem Repetition	52
笏	Wooden Mace	69
祝儀扇	Celebratory Fan	40
障子格子	*Shoji* Grid	56
白衣（しろきぬ）	White Kimono	69
白無垢	White Kimono	62
信玄袋	Large Drawstring Bag	36
末広	Celebratory Fan	63
数寄屋袋	Bag for *Fukusa* Cloth	42
裾	Hem	13
裾回し	*suso-mawashi*	15
青海波	Wave	53
雪駄	Leather-soled Sandals	35
千筋	Thousand Stripe	54
千両	Tilted Wooden Clogs	35
草履	Sandals	34

	袖	Sleeves	13
	袖付	*sode-tsuke*	15
た	太鼓結び	*taiko-musubi*	26
	大名筋	Thin Vertical Stripe	54
	伊達衿	Layered Collar	13
	伊達締め	*datejime*	31
	立涌	Vapor	53
	足袋	*tabi*	33
	袂	Bottom Ends of Sleeves	13
	茶席扇	Tea Ceremony Fan	41
	茶扇子	Tea Ceremony Fan	41
	中啓	Open Celebratory Fan	67
	付け下げ	Informal Kimono	19
	蔦	Ivy	58
	褄	*tsuma*	15
	褄先	*tsuma-saki*	15
	手拭い	Handkerchief	37
	留袖	Formal Kimono for Married Women	16
	共衿	*tomo-eri*	14
な	長襦袢	*naga-juban*	30
	名古屋帯	Semi-formal or Casual Obi	25
	夏扇	Fan	39
	業平格子	Diagonal Grid	57
	鈍色	*nibi-iro*	49
	のめり	Tilted Wooden Clogs	35
は	羽織	Short Coat	65
	羽織紐（白房付き）	Strings with White Tassel	65
	博多帯	Men's Obi	25
	白衣（はくえ）	White Kimono	69
	白扇	Celebratory Fan	40
	肌襦袢	*hada-juban*	30
	鉢巻	Headband	72
	八掛	*hakkake*	15
	縹（花田）色	*hanada-iro*	48
	腹掛け	Apron	73
	半衿	*han-eri*	31
	袢纏	Casual Short Coat	72
	半幅帯	Half-width Obi	25
	檜垣	Cypress Fence	50
	直垂	*Hitatare* Ceremonial Kimono	71
	緋袴	Scarlet Divided Skirt	69
	白衣（びゃくえ）	White Kimono	69

	帛紗（袱紗）	*Fukusa* Cloth	42
	帛紗挟み	Bag for *Fukusa* Cloth	42
	ふくら雀	*fukura-suzume*	26
	袋帯	Formal Obi	25
	藤色	*fuji-iro*	48
	不祝儀扇	Funeral Fan	40
	振り	*furi*	15
	振袖	Formal Kimono for Unmarried Women	17
	風呂敷	Wrapping Cloth	37
	文金高島田	Coiffure for Bride	63
	文庫	*bunko*	27
	紅色（べにいろ）	*beni-iro*	44
	弁柄色	*bengara-iro*	45
	弁慶格子	*Benke* Gingham	57
	棒縞	Bar Stripe	55
	訪問着	Semi-formal Kimono	18
ま	舞扇	Dance Fan	41
	舞扇子	Dance Fan	41
	前身頃	*maemigoro*	15
	丸に梅鉢	Plum Blossoms in Circle	61
	丸に九枚笹	Nine Bamboo Leaves in Circle	59
	丸に剣片喰	Sorrel and Sword in Circle	59
	丸に隅立四ツ目	Four Squares in Circle	60
	丸に橘	Mandarin Orange in Circle	60
	丸に違い鷹羽	Two Feathers Crossing in Circle	61
	丸に三ツ柏	Three Oak Leaves in Circle	60
	丸に横木瓜	Japanese Quince in Circle	61
	万筋	Ten Thousand Stripe	54
	三筋格子	Three Line Grid	56
	身八つ口	*miyatsuguchi*	15
	萌葱（萌黄）色	*moegi-iro*	47
	喪扇	Funeral Fan	40
	股引	Trousers	73
	紋	Family Crest	65
	紋付羽織袴	Formal Kimono for Men	64
や	矢鱈縞	Random Stripe	55
	矢羽根	Arrow Feathers	52
	山吹色	*yamabuki-iro*	46
	浴衣	Casual Summer Kimono	23
	裄	*yuki*	14
	よろけ縞	Wavy Stripe	55
ら	雷	Spiral	53

索引（五十音順）

	利休鼠	*rikyu-nezumi*	49
わ	若竹色	*wakatake-iro*	47
	草鞋	Straw Sandals	73

伝統芸能
JAPANESE TRADITIONAL PERFORMING ARTS

	赤っ面	Red Face	121
あ	揚帽子	Headwear	130
	揚幕（能）	Noh Curtain	93
	揚幕（歌舞伎）	Actor's Curtain	135
	足遣い	Third Puppeteer	113
	厚板	*atsuita*	81
	当帯	*ate-obi*	105
	雨団扇	*ame-uchiwa*	149
	板鬢	Flared Sidelocks	121
	一の松	First Pine Tree	92
	印籠	Lacquered Pill Case	140
	表袴	*uenohakama*	103
	姥	*uba*	85
	綾（老懸）	*oikake*	103
	大鼓	Large Hand Drum	99
	大癋見	*obeshimi*	87
	翁	*okina*	86
	主遣い	Main Puppeteer	112
か	抱え帯	Waistband	123
	鏡板	Back Wall	91
	書割	Background Scenery	132
	楽筝	*gakuso*	108
	楽太鼓	*gaku-daiko*	111
	角火鉢	Brazier	144
	楽琵琶	*gakubiwa*	109
	合掌鏡台	Mirror Stand	144
	鬘帯	*kazura-obi*	77
	裃（上下）	Formal Wear for Samurai	119
	上手	Stage Left	134

	唐織	*karaori*	77
	がり時計	*garidokei*	149
	菊綴	*kikutoji*	79
	階	Stairs	88
	煙管	Tobacco Pipe	138
	煙管筒	Pipe Case	138
	着流し	Kimono without *Hakama*	117
	黄八丈	Striped or Checkered Yellow Kimono	125
	切戸口	Low Sliding Door	95
	隈取（むきみ隈）	*Kumadori* Makeup	119
	黒衿	Black Collar	125
	黒衣	Black Suit	113
	黒御簾	Black Blind	137
	巻纓冠	*ken-ei no kan*	103
	見所	Audience Seats	89
	見台	Bookstand	114
	後見	Understudy	95
	小面	*ko-omote*	84
	腰帯	*koshi-obi*	81
	小鼓	Small Hand Drum	98
	高麗笛	*komabue*	107
さ	酒樽	Sake Barrel	145
	指貫	*sashinuki*	101
	三の松	Third Pine Tree	92
	三歯下駄	Wooden Clogs with Three Platforms	127
	三里当て	Triangular Cloth	121
	地謡	Chorus	94
	糸鞋	*shikai*	101
	しけ	Loose Hair	117
	しごき帯	Waistband	123
	下襲	*shitagasane*	103
	十手	Truncheon	141
	シテ柱	*Shite* Pillar	91
	下手	Stage Right	136
	笏拍子	*shaku-byoshi*	148
	蛇の目傘	Japanese Umbrella	143
	三味線（文楽）	*Shamisen* Players	114
	三味線	*shamisen*	146
	笙	*sho*	106
	尉髪	*jogami*	83
	鉦鼓	*shoko*	110
	定式幕	Main Curtain	133

	すし桶	Sushi Bucket	145
	すっぽん	Runway Stage Lift	137
	摺箔	*surihaku*	77
	迫り	Stage Lift	137
た	太鼓	Large Drum	96
	丈長	*takenaga*	129
	竹本	Narrator and *Shamisen* Player	135
	煙草入れ	Tobacco Pouch	138
	煙草盆	Tobacco Tray	139
	太夫	Narrator	114
	着肉	Body Suit	121
	長絹	*choken*	79
	ちょぼ床	*Takemoto Seat*	135
	丁髷	Men's Topknot	117
	作り物	Stage Set	95
	角隠し	Headwear	130
	つまみ簪	*tsumami-kanzashi*	129
	爪	*tsume*	108
	釣太鼓	*tsuri-daiko*	111
	道中着	*Oiran* Procession Kimono	127
	遠見	Distant Scenery	133
	飛出	*tobide*	87
	鳥甲	*torikabuto*	101
な	長袴	Long Divided Skirt	119
	梨子打烏帽子	*nashiuchi-eboshi*	81
	肉襦袢	Muscle Body Suit	121
	二の松	Second Pine Tree	92
	縫箔	*nuihaku*	79
	根付	Fastener	140
	能管	Flute	97
は	灰吹	Ashtray	139
	白式尉	*hakushikijo*	86
	筥迫	Purse	141
	橋掛り	Corridor	89
	法被	*happi*	81
	花道	Runway	137
	囃子方	Musicians	94
	番傘	Heavy Japanese Umbrella	142
	盤木	*bangi*	148
	半切（はんぎり）	*hangiri*	81
	半切（はんぎれ）	*hangire*	81
	般若	*hannya*	86

	半臂	*hampi*	101
	火入	Kindling Container	139
	引袴	Long Divided Skirt	119
	引幕	Main Curtain	133
	左遣い	Second Puppeteer	113
	篳篥	*hichiriki*	106
	鬢	Sidelocks	117
	びんざさら	*binzasara*	147
	笛	Flute	97
	笛柱	Musicians' Pillar	91
	深井	*fukai*	84
	踏懸	*fugake*	101
	吹き輪銀の前ざし	Silver Hairpin for Princess	123
	ふき綿	Overlay Hem	125
	舞台下駄	Stage Clogs	113
	振り下げ	Hanging Obi Knot	125
	文楽人形	Bunraku Puppet	112
	鼈甲の髪飾り	Tortoiseshell Hair Ornaments	127
	袍	*ho*	101
	本舞台	Main Stage	88
ま	まないた帯	*Oiran* Obi	127
	丸ぐけ	*Maruguke* Obi Belt	123
	廻り舞台	Revolving Stage	132
	御簾	Bamboo Blind	115
	水衣	*mizugoromo*	83
	牟子	*mushi*	105
	胸紐	*munehimo*	79
	紫鉢巻	Purple Headband	131
	紫帽子	Purple Headwear	130
	目付柱	Sighting Pillar	91
	元結（もっとい）	*mottoi*	129
	元結（もとゆい）	*motoyui*	129
や	痩女	*yase-onna*	85
	病鉢巻	Ailing Headband	131
	結綿	*yuiwata*	128
	床	Revolving Stage	115
ら	龍笛	*ryuteki*	107
	陵王面	*ryo-o-men*	105
	襠襠	*ryoto*	105
	艪の音	*ro no oto*	147
わ	ワキ柱	*Waki* Pillar	91

監　修	市田ひろみ　（いちだ・ひろみ）
	服飾評論家・エッセイスト。
	日本和装師会会長などを歴任。2022年逝去。
イラスト	末吉詠子
翻　訳	板井由紀
校　正	Justus WALLEN
デザイン	奥野正次郎（pororoca）

Editorial Supervision	ICHIDA Hiromi
Illustration	SUEYOSHI Eiko
Translation	ITAI Yuki
Proofing	Justus WALLEN
Design	OKUNO Shojiro（pororoca）

英訳付き ニッポンの名前図鑑　和服・伝統芸能

2017年9月19日　初版発行
2025年5月11日　3版発行

編　者　　淡交社編集局
発行者　　伊住公一朗
発行所　　株式会社 淡交社
　　　　　本社　〒603-8588京都市北区堀川通鞍馬口上ル
　　　　　営業　075-432-5156　　編集　075-432-5161
　　　　　支社　〒162-0061東京都新宿区市谷柳町39-1
　　　　　営業　03-5269-7941　　編集　03-5269-1691
　　　　　www.tankosha.co.jp

印刷・製本　　三晃印刷株式会社

©2017 淡交社　Printed in Japan
ISBN978-4-473-04195-1

An Illustrated Guide to Japanese Traditional Clothing and Performing Arts

This book was published in 2017
by Tankosha Publishing Co., Ltd.

定価はカバーに表示してあります。落丁・乱丁本がございましたら、小社書籍営業部宛にお送りください。送料小社負担
にてお取り替えいたします。本書のスキャン、デジタル化等の無断複写は、著作権法上での例外を除き禁じられています。
また、本書を代行業者等の第三者に依頼してスキャンやデジタル化することは、いかなる場合も著作権法違反となります。

シリーズ
英訳付き ニッポンの名前図鑑

和食・年中行事

An Illustrated Guide to Japanese Cooking
and Annual Events

監修　服部幸應

蕎麦湯をつぐ"あの"容器は、なんていう名前？
"曲げわっぱ"ってどんなもの？
"門松"は英語でどのように説明したらいい？
「和食」「食器」「年中行事」にまつわる
モノ・コトの名前を取り上げました。

ISBN 978-4-473-04181-4　　A5判変型 160頁　　本体1,400円＋税